Saws, Planes, *and* Scorps

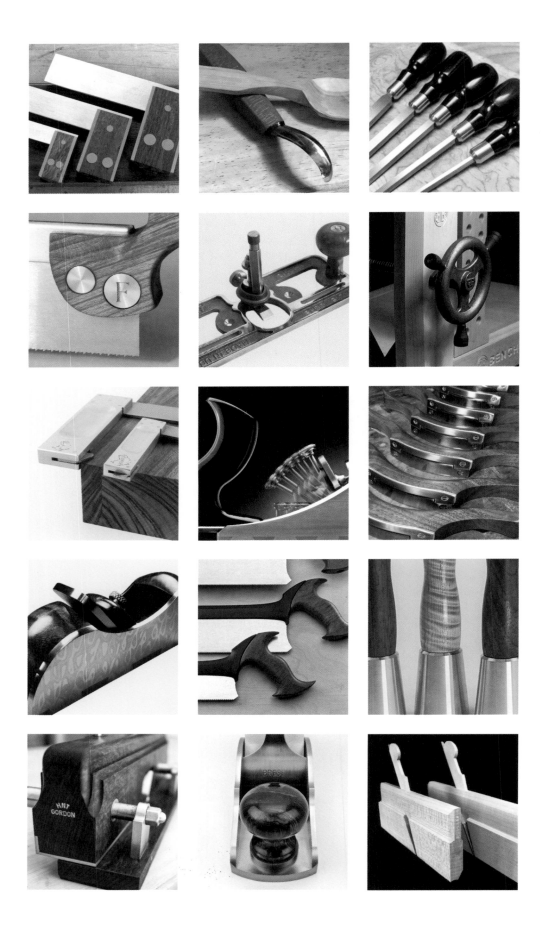

Saws, Planes,
and
Scorps

Exceptional
Woodworking Tools
and Their Makers

David Heim

PRINCETON ARCHITECTURAL PRESS · NEW YORK

Contents

Foreword

It would be possible for an expert joiner to purchase the steel blades and make his own wooden planes; but I feel that it is due to what may be termed "Craft Masonry"—the recognition and respect for skilled workmanship—that makes him reluctant to do so and, instead, to purchase the tools that an unknown fellow-worker has prepared for him with such infinite care. It has never been my experience to meet a tool-maker, but I believe that all joiners must feel how very much their craft depends on the perfection of his skill.

—WALTER ROSE, *The Village Carpenter*

Our tools are extensions of our hands, and we would do well to choose them carefully. Without a finely tuned standard to employ in developing our skills, we are destined to flounder and to fail—never discovering the quality of work that is possible. Every craftsperson needs quality tools.

The spirit of mutual support that Walter Rose describes above is built on a woodworker's deep respect for the rigorous craft of toolmaking, and *Saws, Planes, and Scorps* reminds us that this spirit is alive and well today. We live in a time that has been described as a "hand-tool renaissance"—a day in which backwoodsers and urbanites alike are taking up traditional tools to shape their own piece of the world. In the last decade, the internet has exploded with makers of hand planes featuring custom inlay, backsaws of every possible tooth configuration, and unending varieties of carving knives. If yesterday's problem was finding hand tools worth using, today's is wading through the wealth of available options. There is an overwhelming abundance of phenomenal toolmakers out there today.

And these tools are so good that many sell out in minutes. The makers post small batches of knives or gauges for sale at a scheduled time, and ravenous buyers frantically refresh their browser windows to snatch one before the competition gets it. Only a few people ever make it to the checkout. This insatiable feeding frenzy has created opportunities for new makers to hang out their shingles, and the toolmaking community continues to grow. One would think that this emerging scene would be a cutthroat market, with everyone vying to get to the top of the pack. In fact, these toolmakers embody a form of mutual support and encouragement I've rarely seen anywhere else.

My first experience of this was at Tom Lie-Nielsen's annual open house, where he generously invited makers from around the world to display and sell their tools to his customers. It's one of the most valuable shows of the year for these artisans, and they wouldn't miss it for anything. If that weren't enough, after two busy days of sawdust and shavings, Tom treats everyone to a lobster dinner as thanks for spending the weekend with him. These are the kinds of people that make up the toolmaking community in the twenty-first century.

In a world that seems more and more obsessed with saving a few bucks and finagling free shipping, it would do us well to meet the people behind our purchases. Craftspeople especially long to see the faces behind their tools.

I am blessed to say that many of the makers featured in this book are my personal friends. Watching them pour themselves into their work over the years, I've seen the way they consistently uphold people over profits, quality over quantity. The integrity these makers embody goes beyond the beautiful work of their hands.

I am grateful to David Heim for undertaking such an important task as documenting and celebrating these inspiring makers. His detailed and far-reaching survey will prove to be an immense help to those who are looking for toolmakers worth supporting. And those of us who already own tools made by the folks in this book will gain a deeper appreciation of the skilled workmanship of those committed to putting tools back in the hands of the people.

I'm confident that, in fifty or one hundred years, when woodworkers look back at the early 2000s to see what their craft forebearers were up to, they will see names like Lee Valley, Bad Axe Tool Works, Chris Vesper, and Christopher Schwarz, and they will marvel to see how the commitment to quality work was inseparable from the commitment to quality relationships. Heim's book is a fitting celebration of that mutuality.

JOSHUA A. KLEIN
Founder of *Mortise & Tenon* magazine

Introduction

When I was a very young boy, in the early 1950s, my father owned a small machine shop. As I recall, it had a vertical milling machine, a drill press, a couple of metal lathes, and a powered hacksaw, plus acetylene torches and an arc welder. The place smelled of old grease, hot steel, and oily dust. To a six-year-old kid, it was a wondrous place. I remember once being allowed to use one of the lathes, advancing the cutter to make ribbons of shiny, curly shavings. Like many other wondrous places, though, it wasn't meant to last. My father lost the shop in a fire.

Fast-forward sixty years, when I no longer have a full-time job and I'm wracking my brain for ways to make some money. I hit on a device for people who want to turn wood-bodied pens on a lathe. Most pen-turning equipment holds the wood on a metal shaft called a mandrel, which fits in the lathe's headstock; the tailstock is advanced to squeeze the free end of the mandrel, keeping it centered. Squeeze too much and the mandrel will flex slightly, forcing the wood out of alignment. I figured out a way to keep the mandrel in tension so it wouldn't flex. Thus was born The Better Pen Mandrel.

Despite my early upbringing, I'm no machinist. I found a couple of local shops to make the parts. All I had to do was package the orders, cash the checks, and watch my fortune grow. Or so I thought.

The product itself was the least of it. Marketing my mandrel meant setting up a business with a website, a PayPal account, a bank account, a business license, a sales-tax license, and a fat liability-insurance policy. It meant hiring LegalZoom to file a patent application. It meant contacting the editor of every woodturning magazine and website I could find, imploring them to give my mandrel a review. But most of all, it meant answering a constant stream of questions from potential customers and trying to troubleshoot problems (real or imagined) that they had. After a couple of years of very modest sales, I called it quits.

So as you can see, I'm neither a machinist nor a good business-man. Consequently, I have nothing but unconditional admiration for the makers profiled in this book. They are highly skilled craftsmen and women who take no shortcuts and put the highest premium on quality and precision. They know how to marry high-performance metals with exotic hardwoods to create beautiful tools that also work beautifully. They are visionaries who are determined to take a venerable tool and make it better or to create unique tools that sidestep tradition. Most of these makers are also social-media maestros, with beautiful websites and robust Instagram accounts, Facebook pages, and YouTube channels that attract large numbers of followers.

I wish I could say that I traveled the world in search of great tools, but sadly that wasn't the case. Instead, I typically conducted extensive phone interviews after I immersed myself in a maker's website, blog, and Instagram account. I did conduct in-person interviews with makers who were a reasonable distance from my home in Connecticut. Most of this research happened in late 2019 and early 2020. The makers reviewed the text for accuracy and generously shared nearly all the photos you see.

When I began working on this book, I quickly realized that not all toolmakers are created equal. Some—namely Lie-Nielsen Toolworks, Lee Valley and Veritas Tools, Bridge City Tool Works, and Woodpeckers—are essentially factories with outstanding quality control. I've given them their own chapter in the book because they operate on a different plane from the one- or two-person shops.

Each chapter on individual artisans covers one category of tool—workbenches, hand planes, hammers and chisels, and so on. The text and images introduce the makers who produce the tools I consider the most distinctive, showing how they fabricate their tools, explaining how they decided to start their businesses, and noting what keeps them motivated. I give other makers briefer mentions.

This book represents one woodworker's celebration of splendid, high-quality tools—the output from what I consider the best woodworking hand-tool makers active in North America, Great Britain, Australia, and New Zealand. There are fine toolmakers in other parts of the world, of course, particularly in Japan. But I don't have much to say about Japanese tools in this book, except for notes on workbenches (page 58) and saws (page 86), as these are quite different from their Western counterparts.

Saws, Planes, and Scorps was never meant to be a hand-tool encyclopedia. Let me apologize now to anyone whose work I omitted. That was an oversight, not a snub.

* * *

This book would not have been possible without the enthusiastic cooperation of some seventy toolmakers in six countries. They endured my questions, politely corrected my mistakes, and took time away from bench and forge to scare up the images you see on these pages. Not only do these people make great tools, they help make good books, too.

Thanks also goes to everyone at Princeton Architectural Press for asking me to produce this book and for providing much-needed encouragement as the book took shape.

And, of course, I must thank my wife, Katherine Foran, and my son, Theodore Heim, who tolerated those days when interviews or writing delayed my cooking dinner, mowing the lawn, and countless other chores. I'm always grateful for their patience and understanding.

DAVID HEIM

Prominent Toolworks

I T'S NOT TOO FARFETCHED to say that a round of corporate restructuring in 1975 led to a renaissance in woodworking that has contributed to the success of the four companies profiled here.

The corporation was General Electric, which laid off Paul Roman, who had a job in GE's public affairs department and a longtime interest in woodworking. Rather than pursue another corporate gig, Roman decided to try starting a magazine. He spent six months seeking out the cabinetmakers, woodturners, and other artisans who would become his first authors, and he spent his savings on a mailing to twenty thousand potential customers, asking them to subscribe to a magazine that, in fact, didn't actually exist.

Roman had struck a nerve. He launched *Fine Woodworking* magazine with three thousand subscribers, a number that grew to a hundred thousand in three years' time. Clearly, people were ready for a serious publication written by woodworkers for woodworkers, with advertising limited to products for woodworking.

The magazine's success helped create the market that Lie-Nielsen Toolworks, Lee Valley, Bridge City Tool Works, and Woodpeckers have helped to satisfy. But those four companies endure not just because they're riding a wave, but also because they can deliver accuracy at scale and because they continually innovate. Here's how they do it.

The four companies in this chapter succeed by joining skilled, motivated workers with precision machinery.

TOP: At Lie-Nielsen Toolworks, tools and parts move through the factory in wood crates—a reminder of the toolmaker's days as a blueberry farmer.

ABOVE: These vintage Bridgeport milling machines work alongside more than a dozen new computer numerical control (CNC) machines to produce Lie-Nielsen tools.

Lie-Nielsen Toolworks

Warren, Maine
www.lie-nielsen.com

Nineteen eighty-one was a banner year in the world of woodworking. James Krenov began the woodworking school that now bears his name. *Fine Woodworking* magazine celebrated its sixth year of publishing. And Thomas Lie-Nielsen, a young man selling tools in New York City, decided he wanted to make hand tools instead.

It's no exaggeration to say that Lie-Nielsen's leap into toolmaking opened the current market for high-quality tools from other manufacturers and individual toolmakers.

Lie-Nielsen had had a job at Garrett Wade, a groundbreaking seller of high-quality woodworking tools. When I asked what led him to become a toolmaker, he said, "Guys would come in and complain that they don't make tools like they used to. We also got a lot of people who were looking for a Stanley tool that was no longer made." Stanley sold the No. 95 edge plane from 1911 to 1961. It has a body and sole cast in an L-shape, and is used to plane the edge of a board square to the face. Stanley made its plane from cast iron.

"So I thought, why not make these tools but with better materials, thicker blades, flatter soles, and tight tolerances on the moving parts," Lie-Nielsen continued. "There were a few boutique toolmakers, and they made beautiful things. But most of them didn't last a year. I met one man on Long Island who made an edge plane and who wanted to get out of the business. He was a great machinist, but he wasn't a production guy."

Lie-Nielsen bought the Long Islander's edge-plane business, left Garrett Wade, and moved to a blueberry farm in Maine. He located a foundry to cast the plane's body and additional suppliers for the blades and other parts. Rather than use cast iron, like that for the Stanley No. 95, he chose bronze. Lie-Nielsen handled the polishing and assembly at his kitchen table, after spending the day harvesting berries. "That first summer, there wasn't a lot of time for involvement with tools," he says. Nevertheless, he managed to get his first batch of two hundred planes delivered to Garrett Wade for distribution. He also began to teach himself machining so he could gain control of his manufacturing costs.

In 1983, Lie-Nielsen introduced a bronze-bodied skew-angle block plane, based on the Stanley 140; two years later, a low-angle block plane, modeled after the Stanley 102. He also began placing small classified ads in *Fine Woodworking* magazine. "I was fortunate to have *Fine Woodworking* pave the way, educating and exciting woodworkers about tools and techniques that had been forgotten by the power tool–hungry '50s and '60s," he said in an article marking his company's twenty-fifth anniversary.

Today, Lie-Nielsen Toolworks still sells those three original planes. But its catalog now includes fifteen bench planes, ranging from the miniature No. 1 smoother to the two-foot-long No. 8 jointer; seven block planes; eight joinery planes, including one for creating tongue-and-groove joints; eight saws; four types of chisels, in widths ranging from ⅛ inch to 1 inch; seven types of floats, coarse-toothed tools used to shape mortises; nine screwdrivers; a honing guide; four workbench vises; and a workbench—more than a hundred unique tools in all.

The company's block planes and No. 4 smoothing plane are widely used by professional furniture makers, woodworking teachers, and hobbyists. Those planes are to hand tools what the BMW is to automobiles: reliable, high-performance products priced somewhere below the stratosphere. Lie-Nielsen tells me, "We make tools furniture makers need. Our focus is on tools that make the woodworking job easy. We're not in the luxury tool market."

Lie-Nielsen's original work area on his kitchen table has long since been replaced by a large, well-equipped factory that opened in 1987. The only vestige of his first year as a toolmaker is the shallow wooden crate that holds parts through the production processes; it is the exact size of the ones Lie-Nielsen used when harvesting blueberries. His company uses hundreds of these crates.

As castings and other parts arrive from suppliers, they are logged in and placed in crates. An index card slipped into a sleeve on the end of each crate tracks progress. Workers mark the card to document each stage of manufacturing.

Once logged in, parts move through various stages of work largely done with twenty-seven computer numerical control (CNC) milling machines, twenty-five CNC grinders, a half-dozen vintage Bridgeport milling machines, computer-driven grinders, contraptions that punch sawteeth in a sheet of steel, and a great deal of other machinery. Beginning in 2015, Lie-Nielsen Toolworks began upgrading all its CNC equipment. "The newer ones are significantly more capable," Lie-Nielsen says.

CLOCKWISE FROM TOP LEFT: A CNC machine refines the top edge of a Lie-Nielsen shoulder plane, 0.0015 inches at a time. A Lie-Nielsen worker uses a small pneumatic grinder to smooth the base of a router plane. Brass parts are buffed and polished in a separate wing of the Lie-Nielsen factory. One room in the factory holds equipment to set and sharpen saw teeth.

Castings are fully stress-relieved, a necessary step to ensure the metal won't move. Other machines smooth and polish edges and work surfaces, flatten plane soles and plane irons, grind the edge on chip breakers, and sharpen the bevel on plane irons. More CNC machines rough-cut wood saw handles and turn chisel handles. Workers do the final shaping and smoothing at a half-dozen mini-lathes outfitted with a tubular sanding sleeve. The lathes are mounted at an angle to make it easier for the workers to reach into nooks and crannies. The bronze-bodied products have their own space, where workers seated at buffing machines give the parts their high polish.

Despite the presence of so much computer-driven machinery, Lie-Nielsen says, "We are not automated in any sense." By that, he means that the workers' eye and judgment are critical at every stage of production. The day I visited the factory, for example, I saw some router-plane bodies with near-invisible imperfections outlined on the soles with black marker. Two workers were carefully regrinding the soles in a CNC machine, half a thousandth of an inch at a pass, to erase the flaws. Nearby, other workers were lapping plane irons by hand, passing them over abrasive paper adhered to a dead-flat slab of metal.

The Lie-Nielsen name is probably as well known today as the Stanley name was in its heyday. That's due in large part to the company's regular program of Hand Tool Events. These weekend shows held around the country—there were sixteen scheduled for 2020—are not just a showcase for Lie-Nielsen's tools; they also allow other toolmakers to show off their products. Recent guest presenters included Red Rose Reproductions (page 140), Plate 11 Woodworking (page 42), and Voigt Planes (page 136).

The company also runs regular weekend workshops at its headquarters. Workshops have included how to make molding planes with Matt Bickford (page 128); making a cabriole leg with Aspen Golann, a graduate of the North Bennet Street School who now works in North Carolina; and precision with hand planes, featuring the famed cabinetmaker Garrett Hack. Many of the workshops are sold out months in advance.

"The hand-tool market has a lot of beginners, and we spend a lot of time teaching," Lie-Nielsen says. This includes in-person demonstrations as well as dozens of videos. And since his company sells edge tools, it spends a good deal of time showing people how to keep those edges in condition. "We teach a sharpening technique that you can use and succeed with," Lie-Nielsen says.

Lie-Nielsen, his company's vice president, Robin Nolan, and I spoke in a spacious second-floor office. Fittingly, Lie-Nielsen sat at one of his company's workbenches, next to his desk. A large plan for a wooden boat hangs on one wall. Shelves along one wall hold some Stanley tools as well as prototypes of some Lie-Nielsen tools.

I asked how the company's first tools compare with the tools made today. "The edge plane is not much different," Lie-Nielsen said, "but the low-angle block plane is way better now."

Later he told me, "We've had a quality increase over the last few years, so we get better results with less work." He said, "I do a lot of telling people what to do, based on my experience. Toolmaking is my real love, but I do like the variety of getting deeply involved in one thing or another." At present, he's doing a deep dive into grinding, to make that stage of manufacturing more precise and efficient.

"As a rule, I have not hired experienced people," Lie-Nielsen says. "They often don't have a lot of interest in learning new things." By contrast, he tells me about a young man he hired six or seven years ago. "He said he'd mow the lawn, he wanted to work here that badly," Lie-Nielsen says. The man started at the bottom and now, still in his twenties, he supervises thirty-five people and has learned machining.

The company's last new tool was a honing guide, introduced in 2015. But more are still to come. "I still have a number of tools I'm interested in," Lie-Nielsen says. "We're focused on what tools furniture makers need. We cover a lot, but not everything. It's partly dependent on what falls in place, partly on what I feel is appropriate for us to make. We focus on tools that make the woodworking job easy, tools people can succeed with."

LEFT: "Toolmaking is my real love," says Thomas Lie-Nielsen, who has been doing what he loves for more than forty years.

BELOW: The Lie-Nielsen showroom at its Maine headquarters invites visitors to touch and try the tools.

Lee Valley and Veritas Tools

Ottawa, Ontario, Canada
www.leevalley.com/en-ca
www.veritastools.com

I own a four-inch double square. It's the tool I use to check the thickness of wood after running pieces through the planer, to set my table saw's blade height, and to mark a board where I want to rip it to width. The square is graduated in sixty-fourths of an inch (which is usually four times more accuracy than I can handle).

The square is one of fourteen hundred products designed and made by Veritas Tools, the design and manufacturing arm of Canada's Lee Valley Tools. The late Leonard Lee founded Lee Valley in 1976, selling kits to make wood stoves from metal barrels. The company has grown steadily over the decades. It launched Veritas Tools in 1982 with a dovetail marker. Its first unique plane, a low-angle block plane, came on the market in 1992.

Today, Lee Valley has 850 full-time employees and a thriving retail business, selling woodworking tools, gardening tools, kitchen tools, and cabinet hardware by mail and online as well as at a network of twenty retail stores across Canada and the United States.

Veritas makes tools in two facilities, both highly automated. The company is beginning to implement a system where products move on conveyors from one milling machine to the next. "We can load up to twenty-four hours' worth of work and walk away from it," says Robin Lee, the founder's son and current chief executive. He adds that Veritas "has been at one hundred percent of capacity for far longer than I care to admit," making more than one million parts each year.

At present, the company has a three-year backlog of tools awaiting manufacture. "That gives us a fair amount of time to think about what we're doing," Lee says. "I'll be the first to admit that we didn't pay enough attention to aesthetics when we initially started. I have called our first planes the East German swimmers of the tool world: they performed well but were clunky and chunky."

No one would accuse the company's DX60 block plane of being clunky. In profile, the plane looks as much like a streamlined race car as it does a shop tool. Cast from nickel-resist ductile iron (a metal containing a lot of chrome), the plane body has swept-back recesses on the sides,

TOP: Lee Valley and Veritas Tools rely on highly automated equipment to produce their tools. Here, a CNC machine refines the casting for the body of a hand plane.

ABOVE: The company is known for reinterpreting and updating classic tools into new products, such as its DX60 block plane.

which provide convenient places for your fingers. The curved lever cap makes a perfect place to put your palm.

New products come to market in one of three ways. As Lee explains it to me, "One, planned activity. We have a strategic plan for products, and it relates to our machinery and our production capability. A lot of our forward planning is designed to stretch our capacity. Two is a reaction. For example, when Record [a company founded in Sheffield, England] stopped making tools, we lost a major supplier, so we had to realign. Three is that lightbulb moment when we have an idea and say, 'We're going to go there,' and leverage our product development."

Product designers make use of the company's collection of one hundred thousand tools. "It's our physical library," Lee says. "We'll get an old tool into our hands to see what the balance is like and how it performs. There's always an opportunity to examine an existing tool but design from first principles. We address function first." But Veritas designers are also concerned with maintaining "trade dress"—the visual style of a tool. "If you see a red anodized aluminum tool, you know whose it is," he says, in an obvious reference to Woodpeckers (page 30).

Tool design "is not a question of reproduction," Lee says. "We have to place the tool in context of how people work today. We have to understand how people are going to use the product. We're often recasting the context of a traditional tool. It's important to know why we're making a tool. It's so easy to make something different, but there has to be a purpose for it."

He cites the company's new line of flushing chisels, which are based on patternmaker's chisels from the company's collection. Today, they're used to trim inlay, clean up corners, and extend a surface. A single handle threads onto one of four blades; the socket for the blade is on the top face of the blade, so the handle is offset. The Veritas website explains, "One hand pushes the tool while your other hand guides the blade along the workpiece, giving you fine control with a comfortable grip."

Or consider the Veritas dovetail saw. Like other such saws, this one is backed, or stiffened, with a strip of material along the top. In place of the traditional brass strip is a backing material that consists of stainless-steel powder for weight and glass fibers for stiffness, held together with a polymer resin binder. The back is formed over the saw plate as well as the top of the tote, or handle. A threaded rod goes through the tote and into a boss at the end of the spine to hold the tote in place. It's an innovative design that eliminates the split bolt connecting plate and tote on a traditional saw. It's probably easier to manufacture and easier to assemble than a conventional saw.

CLOCKWISE FROM TOP LEFT: Lee Valley has a "physical library" of one hundred thousand tools, including this set of old flushing chisels. The company's new flushing chisels are easy to guide for accurate trimming. Lee Valley's backed saws replace a conventional metal back with one made of a composite material that helps hold the handle and blade together.

LEFT: Veritas Tools's look, or "trade dress," extends to its product packaging and design.

RIGHT: One of the high-tech setups that Lee Valley and Veritas Tools use for quality control.

Once the company decides to move forward with a new tool, Lee says, it's modeled and prototyped. "It's important to get the design into three dimensions as soon as possible." That way, Veritas can enlist its customers to give the new tool a thorough test drive.

"Our customers are our focus group," Lee says. "It's important to have that tight connection between retail and manufacturing." The company connects customers with designers directly to go over how a tool is used or problems with its use. In some cases, it may give groups of customers three products, each slightly different, to test ergonomics. The company also sends designers to tool shows to gather feedback. For all that, however, Lee says, "We don't design by committee. We do our testing to validate a product."

"We've always been your grandfather's tool store or your father's tool store," Lee says. "Now we want to be your son's or daughter's tool store as well. It's important to get kids to buy into the idea that you don't have to buy a solution. We're teaching people that they don't just have to buy things. They can make things. It's most important to open people's eyes to the possibilities. Lee Valley is keying more on the promotion of craft— the ability to work with your hands and modify your environment. We want to support craft at all levels." The Lee Valley stores have crafts for kids every weekend. "It's not necessarily woodworking," Lee explains. "It might be burning a design on leather or making a keychain."

Lee also says, "I don't want to train people to buy stuff they don't need. I tell my sales staff to talk people out of buying things. We make very high-end products in very small quantities. Our aim is not to grow as fast as possible, but to grow as sustainably as possible."

Bridge City Tool Works
Montclair, California
bridgecitytools.com

Born and raised in Iowa, John Economaki bailed out of engineering school and moved to Portland, Oregon, in 1973 to take a job as a high school shop teacher. After doing that for six years, he spent a summer vacation at the Anderson Ranch Arts Center, in Snowmass Village, Colorado, taking a furniture-making class with the legendary Sam Maloof. This was the first of several "vector bumps" in Economaki's life— his term for experiences that fling a person in a new direction.

Watching Maloof—a largely self-taught furniture maker whose most enduring work is a rocking chair made of sinuous parts—Economaki says he knew then that he wanted to become a furniture maker too.

He began designing and building furniture at night in the school shop and, a year after studying with Maloof, stopped teaching and took up furniture making full time. Economaki says that he was "blinded by both passion and ignorance."

In 1983, another vector bump struck. "I went to bed one night and woke up the next day with an allergic reaction to wood dust," he tells me. The furniture making came to a halt at a time when he had four apprentices working for him and a three-year backlog of orders. "After I refunded all the deposits, I had a couple of thousand dollars left," he recalls. He plowed that into a toolmaking enterprise.

His first tool was a try square, a nod back to his early days as a shop teacher. Dismayed at the poor quality of the squares the school bought for the shop, he had his class make better ones.

"Back then, the only way to get a 'square' square was to buy a machinist's square," he tells me. "The woodworking squares were crap. They cost two dollars. We did a rosewood and brass square and charged forty-five dollars. The response was literally unbelievable." Bridge City Tool Works (after one of Portland's nicknames) was born.

The country was in a recession in the early 1980s. "That's the best time to start a business," Economaki says. "If you can make it then, you're going to have a good time when things improve." That was certainly true for Bridge City Tool Works.

ABOVE: The sinuous foxtail adjustment lever of this shoulder plane is a reminder of John Economaki's first encounter with a wild fox.

RIGHT: When a severe allergy halted Economaki's woodworking career, he shifted to toolmaking. He has produced a new tool every couple of months for thirty years.

Economaki says he sold three thousand dollars' worth of tools in 1983. The next year, he says, sales jumped to $35,000. Then to $100,000 the next year. "Our sales doubled every year until 1990, when we had $5 million in sales," he says.

Economaki produced new tools at a torrential pace—hand planes, squares, marking gauges, drills, mallets, awls, and various multipurpose tools. In 2013 he wrote, "We have introduced a new product, on average, every eight to ten weeks over the past 30 years." He wrote that in *Quality Is Contagious: John Economaki & Bridge City Tool Works*, a catalog produced for a retrospective exhibition of his tools and furniture at Portland's Museum of Contemporary Craft. The book's photographs were shot by Joe Felzman, Economaki's longtime collaborator.

His thought process seems to begin with the essence of a tool. When designing a bench plane, for instance, he begins by recognizing that a woodworker sometimes needs a plane with a high-angle iron (aka the blade) to smooth wild-grained woods and a low-angle iron for straight grain. Then he questions that basic principle. "Why have two planes?" he'll ask himself. "Why can't the iron be adjustable?" And he will set out to perfect a plane with an adjustable iron. He introduced one in 2005, with brass sides dovetailed into a stainless-steel sole, and a frog—the iron's support—that pivots as it moves in a slot in the sole to set the blade angle.

The next year, Economaki reinvented the shoulder plane, replacing the typical blade-adjustment knob with a lever he calls a foxtail. "I found the inspiration after my first encounter with a wild fox. I was completely gobsmacked by the beauty of this animal and its fluffy tail," he wrote in *Quality Is Contagious*. "I realized that it would be possible to create a new kind of shoulder plane.... The stylized Foxtail grip lifts up and unlocks the blade. This is one of my favorite designs as it works in all positions, including lying on its side."

Economaki says his most important tool is the Jointmaker Pro, introduced in 2009. Think of it as a hand-powered table saw, but with a Japanese-style hand-saw blade instead of a circular one. It allows the user to make precision cuts—to within a thousandth of an inch, Economaki says—at any angle.

The Jointmaker Pro's genesis was a simpler tool that clamped to the end of a board to guide a saw. Economaki created it for a woodworker who suffered from Parkinson's disease. "No matter how much he would shake, the joint maker would guide the cut," he tells me. "He could now cut dovetails."

Then Economaki clamped a Japanese pull saw in a vise and dragged a dowel over it. Impressed with how easily he could cut the dowel, he began working on a tool with a stationary blade and a way to move stock over it. "A year later and four hundred thousand dollars in prototypes, we had a working tool," he says.

Of the Jointmaker Pro, or JMP, Economaki wrote, "One of the more exciting aspects of this tool is the appeal to those with disabilities that prevent them from using hand saws. The JMP allows them to produce high-quality joinery so they can continue to pursue their woodworking passion."

Economaki's concern for people with disabilities extends to the design of other Bridge City tools. The adjustable square and some adjustable planes have easily manipulated locking levers instead of small knobs, for example. Economaki calls this "an ergonomic improvement for those with disabilities, a group I had ignorantly ignored until arthritis found a home in my hands."

Bridge City now sells tools—twenty-six separate tools, and the list is growing—in some five dozen countries. The lineup includes the Jointmaker Pro, the Chopstick Master (a fixture to hold thin wood as you use a small plane to shape a chopstick), three bench planes, an assortment of layout tools, and a small line of Japanese-style hand saws.

By 2001, Bridge City Tool Works had more than sixty employees working in a brand new 25,000-square-foot facility. Then September 11 delivered another vector bump. "The phones stopped ringing. We had never had a day with no sales calls, but now we had six days in a row," Economaki says. "I had eleven 800 lines, and none of them were ringing."

Economaki was forced to sell control of Bridge City Tool Works, and he stopped manufacturing. "I went to an outsourcing model," he says, adding that he had grown tired of supervising the manufacturing crew.

He says that outsourcing provided a formula where "I could succeed with three or four people." That worked for a while, until two of his employees quit. So, in 2013, he began a business relationship with Harvey Industries, a large manufacturer based in China. It became Bridge City's licensed toolmaker in 2013 and acquired Bridge City in 2018.

When Harvey Industries took over Bridge City, Economaki agreed to stay on for two years as the designer in chief. That arrangement ended in June 2020. Economaki's plans for life after Bridge City? "If all goes according to plan," he told me in March 2020, "I'll tear down my garage and build a new one. I'll open a free school for kids to teach them how to make cool stuff. And in my spare time, I'll pursue my unbelievably crazy passion for bird photography."

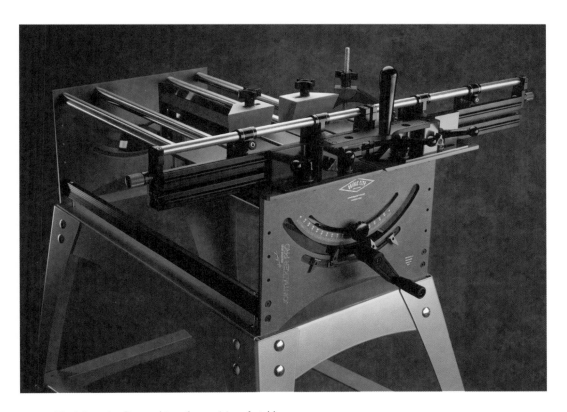

The Jointmaker Pro combines the precision of a table
saw with the finesse of a Japanese hand saw to make
accurate cuts at any angle. Economaki says it's his most
important tool.

Woodpeckers

Strongsville, Ohio
www.woodpeck.com

I first encountered Woodpeckers in 2014, when I demonstrated the SketchUp design program at a series of weekend expositions known as the Woodworking Shows. The shows' exhibitors traveled to thirteen cities, setting up each weekend in a fairgrounds building or a small exposition center. The shows were almost always packed with spectators who came to look at and buy everything from router bits to books to band saws. The halls rang with the noise of a hundred conversations and the roar of machinery. In the midst of it all was the Woodpeckers booth, usually crowded with customers. In the center of the booth was Kathy Hummel. Unfailingly patient and cheerful, she showed off the company's products, answered questions, and made change.

She helped found Woodpeckers with her husband, Richard. When I spoke with Richard for this book, he said, "My wife is integral to the business. I worked the trade shows for ten years, but she's done it for twenty. She's by far the best salesperson we've had."

Richard Hummel calls the launch of Woodpeckers "the culmination of my career as a woodworking hobbyist." He had a day job in computer software and worked in his woodshop on evenings. "I had drying racks in my shop, and I'd built a kiln. I wanted tools but couldn't afford them. So some relatives of mine in Germany sent me some tools to use and extras to sell to make some money. I started selling tools off my porch."

Kathy Hummel came up with the Woodpeckers name and, for his birthday, commissioned a graphic artist to come up with a logo. "It kind of stuck," says Richard.

In 1990, Hummel lost his computer job. "I discussed the situation with my wife—to get a real job or do this," meaning full-time tool sales. "We decided to do this."

Through the 1990s, Woodpeckers mainly handled other companies' tools. The first Woodpeckers-produced product was a router lift. The Hummels outsourced the machining for that one. Hummel then bought a milling machine, "which I did not know how to run," he says. But that purchase launched Woodpeckers as a manufacturer as well as a retailer.

Woodpeckers, which started as a modest tool-selling business, is now a major tool manufacturer, operating from this large plant in a Cleveland suburb.

Today, Woodpeckers makes nearly everything it sells (it still retails some other companies' products, including clamps, router bits, and table-saw blades). Most of the tools Woodpeckers makes are for layout: rulers, squares, gauge blocks, templates for drilling shelf-pin holes, and so on. It also still makes router tables, router lifts, slab-flattening mills, and a growing line of clamping tools. In all, it makes more than four hundred unique tools.

Hummel emphasizes the accuracy of Woodpeckers tools. "For some time, measuring and layout tools were a major part of our existence," Hummel tells me. "The eternal challenge is making a square. We've made hundreds of thousands of them and spent millions of dollars on equipment to make a good square. How good does a square need to be? I say it should be an order of magnitude better than the material you're working with. Our tolerance is 90 degrees within 0.0085 degrees. That's ten times better than an off-the-shelf square."

The company operates from an 86,000-square-foot building in a Cleveland suburb. It has 115 employees and some 50 machines—CNC mills, lathes, and Swiss lathes (they have a traveling headstock and so can turn something ⅛ inch in diameter and 2 feet long, Hummel says).

CLOCKWISE FROM TOP LEFT:
New Woodpeckers products begin as 3D computer models and prototypes. Pressing the handle onto one of the company's signature squares. A router lift, the first Woodpeckers product, is still manufactured. A worker unscrews a batch of freshly machined blades for squares.

You can recognize a Woodpeckers product from across the room. It's often made from aircraft aluminum or stainless steel, laser-etched with the necessary scales and markings. The aluminum is anodized a bright red. That's the "trade dress" mentioned by Robin Lee of Lee Valley. (Curiously, Hummel says he doesn't remember when he switched from the company's original gold anodizing to red. He just recalls that he got bored with the gold.)

The red anodizing isn't the only thing that sets Woodpeckers apart. Since 2010, it has made what it calls OneTIME tools: unique products sold for only a few weeks. These include layout and measuring tools, routing accessories, and re-creations of century-old hand tools. The first OneTIME tool was a set of small T-squares with holes for a pencil point every ½ inch, for laying out various types of joints.

"The OneTIME tool program is really important to our history," Hummel says. "There are a lot of tools we want to make. Typically, you make a tool and try to guess how many you're going to sell. This ties up resources. But the OneTIME tool program lets us make whatever we want. Three weeks later it's dead and gone and we're on to the next thing. We don't care how many we sell. And I think woodworkers like the program because there's always something new."

In most cases, the engineers at Woodpeckers generate the ideas for some of these tools on their own; in other cases, the company develops the tool based on a proposal from a woodworker.

Hummel says Woodpeckers can develop a OneTIME tool in as little as three months, but it typically takes six to nine months to refine the design and make a series of prototypes. The company dedicates eight CNC machines just for prototyping to support the thirteen engineers working to develop new tools. "There's a standing joke in the building that ideas are worth nothing," Hummel says. "Ideas are the easy part. In a typical iteration, we'll make ten or eleven bad ones before we get to the twelfth, which is what we want."

In recent years, Woodpeckers has begun to branch out from tools for measuring, marking, and setup. In 2017, it introduced its Ultra-Shear line of woodturning tools. These cut with a long-lasting carbide insert that's exceptionally sharp and easy to replace. The line includes tools with round, square, and diamond-shaped inserts, in three sizes. There's also a pen mandrel and pen mill that I wish I had invented.

In 2019, Woodpeckers bought Blue Spruce Toolworks (page 68), which makes high-end chisels, mallets, squares, and bevel gauges, as well as a marking-tool system with a dozen different blades. It was the company's first acquisition, and it puts Woodpeckers in competition with the likes of Lee Valley and Lie-Nielsen. But Hummel says he's not concerned. "While demonstrating at shows, I spent ten years competing with companies that wanted to eat my lunch," he told me. "I think we all do better when consumers have choices. And there are good choices out there. Lee Valley makes great products. Lie-Nielsen makes great products. Competition doesn't bug me a bit."

As for the future, Hummel has this to say: "If it involves woodworking and is hobbyist related, that's the direction we will go. I don't have any interest in making tools for Home Depot, and I don't want to make tools for industrial shops. But if it's a woodworking tool that a serious hobbyist or custom-furniture maker might be interested in, it's fair game."

Workbenches

A GOOD, STOUT WORKBENCH sits at the heart of every serious woodworker's shop. More than just an oversized table, the bench is an essential tool. A good bench has a vise—or, more commonly, two vises—as well as various devices to hold a board when you plane, chisel, or saw it. These often include one or more bench dogs, pegs that fit into holes in the top; a deadman, a sliding board mounted vertically below the benchtop, with pegs to support the free end of a board clamped in a vise on the front of the bench; and a holdfast, a piece of iron shaped like an upside-down L, that fits into a hole in the top of the bench so it bears down on the work.

Carpenters and cabinetmakers in Europe have used benches and bench dogs at least as far back as Roman times. Bench designs evolved as woodworkers shifted from using green wood (best shaped with adzes and knives) to seasoned timber shaped with saws, chisels, and hand planes. The rise of guilds and their monopoly on specific trades also helped foster specialization in bench design.

According to *The Workbench Book* by Scott Landis, a workbench with a vise made its first known appearance in a 1505 engraving. By the eighteenth century, carpenters, cabinetmakers, and joiners throughout Europe were using benches that would seem right at home in many modern shops. (Japanese woodworkers use a very different type of bench, as you can see in the text on page 58.) Those vintage European benches generally followed three basic designs.

The first, sometimes called the German or Scandinavian style, had a shoulder vise on the left front corner of the bench, a tail vise at the opposite end, and a row of bench-dog holes aligned with the tail vise. Tage Frid, a longtime woodworking instructor at the Rhode Island School of Design and an early contributing editor to *Fine Woodworking* magazine, popularized this style through his teaching and writing. It has become the model for many of today's factory-made benches.

The second design, described by the Englishman Joseph Moxon in his 1703 book *Mechanick Exercises*, is a beefy bench outfitted with a twin-screw vise. Cabinetmakers and carpenters in colonial America used

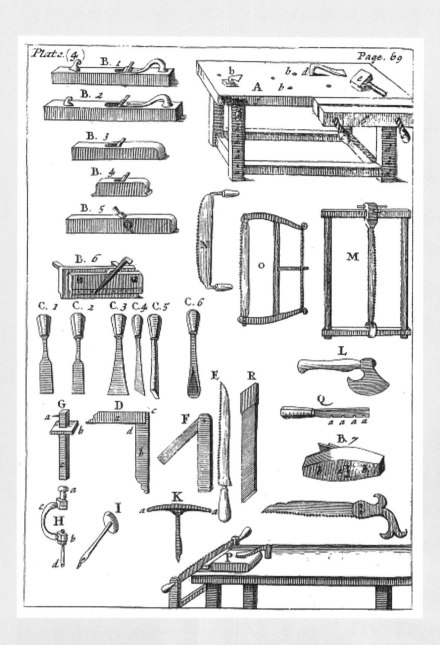

In this plate from a 1703 treatise on woodworking,
Joseph Moxon illustrates a range of tools—and
a twin-screw bench vise—that are used to this day.

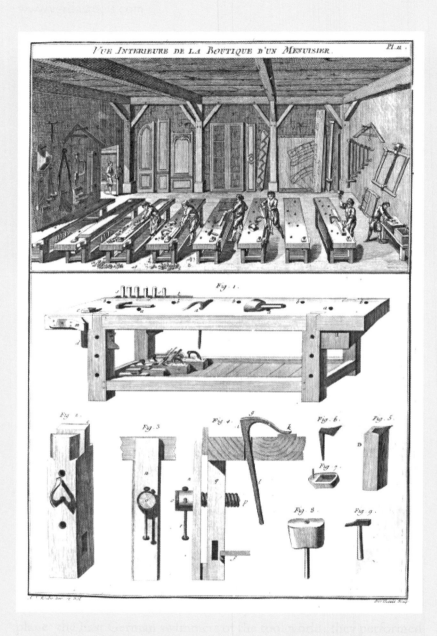

The type of bench that André-Jacob Roubo depicted
in this 1774 drawing is still used today by a large army
of devotees who favor its size and weight.

benches similar to the one Moxon depicted. Moxon's name endures in the form of an auxiliary two-screw vise clamped to the bench top and used for sawing dovetails and other detail work.

The third, popularized by André-Jacob Roubo in his seminal book *L'art du menuisier* (1774), had a vertical vise fitted to one of the bench's four massive legs. Holes on the bench top as well as on other legs allowed workers to use holdfasts to secure boards on edge or flat for sawing, planing, and jointing. The Roubo bench also incorporated a planing stop (a large bench dog fitted with a saw-toothed piece of metal) and a *crochet* (a stop attached to the front corner of the top). The top on a Roubo bench consists of two slabs, each five to six inches thick and typically nine feet long. Timbers that massive are now as rare as the ivory-billed woodpecker, so most bench makers get the timbers they need by gluing up thinner pieces. These days, a narrow space between the slabs serves as a toolholder or a space to fit clamps.

Today, a woodworker in the United States can quickly build a serviceable bench from a couple of sheets of plywood or a stack of common construction lumber and bolt on a small cast-iron vise. Those with more ambition can attach a ready-made top to shop-made hardwood trestles, or build a bench totally to their liking, most likely adapting one of the vintage designs from the 1700s or 1800s. In the United States, only a few companies specialize in custom-made benches. The Roubo style prevails.

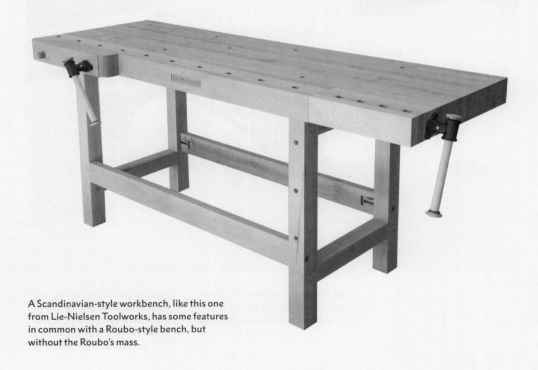

A Scandinavian-style workbench, like this one from Lie-Nielsen Toolworks, has some features in common with a Roubo-style bench, but without the Roubo's mass.

Benchcrafted
Cedar Rapids, Iowa
www.benchcrafted.com

Benchcrafted is a family-run company that started by making what it calls the Mag-Blok. It's a length of wood with embedded magnets; screw the block to a wall and it will hold just about any iron or steel item, from a paring knife to a jack plane. In 2008, two years after it debuted the Mag-Blok, Benchcrafted began making workbench hardware. The company's main offering is an updated leg vise for a Roubo-style bench. It has a heavy handwheel that can open or close the vise rapidly, plus a scissor mechanism to keep the jaw (also called a chop) parallel to the bench leg.

In addition to the hardware, Benchcrafted makes complete benches and sells plans for those who want to build their own. The basic bench has only a leg vise. You can order kits for a Moxon vise, a Hi-Vise that clamps to the bench top, and a tail vise, also called a wagon vise. With a wagon vise, turning the screw moves a dog-hole block rather than the chop.

As small toolmakers go, Benchcrafted is a big deal. The company organizes the Handworks show, a major semiannual event that brings thousands of hand-tool makers and users to Iowa for two days of buying, selling, swapping, and camaraderie. It also organizes the French Oak Roubo Project, or FORP, a weeklong bench-building exercise (see page 50). The most recent FORP, in 2019, resulted in the construction of twenty benches.

Jameel Abraham, who runs Benchcrafted with his brother Father John Abraham, has been doing what he calls serious woodworking since he was in high school. "I was always searching for ways to do things better. I started designing vises based on how I like to work," he tells me. "The bench grew out of our vise production and design."

The Abrahams have a handful of employees and want to keep the company small. "We're motivated by one thing; making the best, most satisfying things we can," they say on the Benchcrafted website.

TOP: Benchcrafted sells fully assembled Roubo-style benches as well as innovative hardware for the bench vises.

ABOVE: Turning the screw on a Benchcrafted tail vise moves a bench-dog hole block back and forth.

ABOVE: Benchcrafted's scissor mechanism keeps the jaw, or chop, of the vise parallel to the leg as it moves in and out.

RIGHT: Benchcrafted is a family-run business that operates from a small facility in Cedar Rapids, Iowa.

Jameel Abraham manages Benchcrafted with his brother Father John. "I'm a woodworker who designs vises and benches," he says.

"We aren't interested in getting rich," Jameel Abraham tells me. "We just want to make an honest living. We like to keep things small and intimate so we can focus on product design. Our life and culture are engrossed in woodworking all the time. I don't consider myself a businessman. Instead, I say that I'm a woodworker who designs vises and benches."

Benchcrafted settled on the Roubo design, Abraham says, because "the French bench offers the most efficiency and versatility." For a bench builder, however, a Roubo presents some major challenges, beginning with the need for wood five to six inches thick. "It's difficult to source slabs of thick, monolithic woods," says Abraham. So, like most Roubo makers, Benchcrafted laminates two-inch-thick pieces of North American rock maple for the top and legs.

Workers connect legs and stretchers with drawbored mortise-and-tenon joints. That's a venerable technique; drawboring forces a dowel through slightly misaligned holes, so the leg and stretcher come together tightly. A drawbored joint can stay together without glue. "It's as solid as humans can make it, short of growing a tree in the shape of a bench," says the company's website.

Thick pieces of wood, even though dry on the outside, can still be wet in the center, which presents another challenge for the bench maker. As Abraham explains, "You build a bench, put the legs on it, and let it settle down. The wood will move quite a lot in the first year." The top must be planed flat. "But then a kind of skin forms over it," Abraham says. "Even if the wood is still wet in the middle, it will be stable on the outside."

Plate 11 Woodworking

Ozark, Missouri

www.plate11.com

Anyone who knows anything about Roubo benches will immediately understand how Plate 11 Woodworking got its name. It's a reference to an engraving in Roubo's *L'art du menuisier* that details a bench.

Mark Hicks, Plate 11's owner, explains how he got into the workbench business. "I came at this with no hand-tool experience," he says. "I had been building furniture using only power tools." He spent nine frustrating years running a production furniture business that he took over from a relative. "I had read Christopher Schwarz's book *The Anarchist's Tool Chest*, and the part about work holding made sense to me," he says. (In his book, Schwarz maintains that all benches should let you hold the wood so you can easily work on the faces, edges, and ends.) Hicks adds, "I decided I wanted this for myself. Thinking about four-inch-thick parts blew my mind, though. We didn't order even two-inch-thick lumber for our furniture."

Then Hicks took a furniture-making class with Schwarz, the premier Roubo-bench devotee. The German-style benches at the school proved difficult to use, Hicks tells me. "Students are a lot like employees. They don't treat the equipment well." Not only did the tail vises sag, the bench design made it difficult to position clamps for a glue-up.

"It was put to me by Chris that I should make a bench for other people. I thought that if I liked it, others would also like it." Schwarz offered to display a prototype of Hicks's bench at that year's Handworks event. "There were two weeks between the end of the class and the beginning of Handworks, so I had a week to get the material and a week to make the prototype," Hicks says. That first bench, made from beech, lacked the Roubo's signature leg vise. And glue. "We put it together dry for the display. It was humid at Handworks, so of course the bench swelled up and locked itself together. We had to knock it apart."

Despite those problems, Hicks's benches found a following, and his manufacturing skills improved. "I was using hand tools too often to be profitable. I was cutting mortises by hand, when I should have made a router jig, drilled out a lot of the waste, and routed the mortise." Now, he says, "I'm always looking for some efficiency."

TOP: A bench from Plate 11 Woodworking follows the classic split-top Roubo design, but uses different woods on the vises and deadman for contrast.

ABOVE LEFT: Plate 11 builds its benches from thick pieces of silver maple.

ABOVE CENTER: Gluing up the top requires several clamps and metal cauls to keep the assembly square.

ABOVE RIGHT: This view of an upended Plate 11 bench clearly shows its thick legs and stretchers, assembled with dovetailed tenons and drawbored joints to make it rock steady.

Today, he sells custom-made Roubo benches as well as shave horses and shave-horse plans. He also leads frequent bench-building classes at his shop in Ozark, Missouri. Hicks typically uses Benchcrafted hardware for his vises.

A basic bench, seven feet long with a de rigueur split top, is made from silver maple, with contrasting hardwoods available to be used for the chop on the leg vise and the end of the tail vise. They aren't cheap. "You can spend as much as $10,000 on a bench," Hicks says.

RIGHT: The space between the halves of a split-top Roubo bench is a convenient place to hold tools.

BELOW: Contrasting woods add a strong decorative detail, and deep dovetails hold the tail vise securely.

Profile: Christopher Schwarz

He doesn't care for the term, but Christopher Schwarz is very much an influencer. In preparing this book, I encountered several toolmakers who told me that Schwarz's book *The Anarchist's Tool Chest* changed their approach to woodworking; others said that their business took off once Schwarz mentioned their tools on his blog; still others said that Schwarz's teaching inspired them.

Schwarz tells me he never set out to be an influencer. "I was always a writer working in the background. I'm not an attention-getter or an attention-seeker." He says that he appreciates the notoriety he receives, but accepts it very reluctantly. "I'm very much an introvert," he says.

Schwarz was associated with *Popular Woodworking* magazine for close to twenty years. He picked up his own notoriety with the 2010 publication of *The Anarchist's Tool Chest*. Part personal history, part screed promoting hand tools, part how-to, the book steered countless hobbyists away from motorized woodworking machinery. He gave readers a list of essential hand tools as well as instructions for building his anarchist's tool chest.

I'm sure that the book also helped grow the audience for Schwarz's blog, where he writes about upcoming projects and classes and publicizes tools (and their makers) that he favors. And because Schwarz regularly travels around the United States and Europe to teach, he has plenty of opportunities to hear from would-be toolmakers.

A case in point is Chris Kuehn, who now runs Sterling Tool Works (page 162). In 2013, he had just earned an MBA degree and treated himself to a class at Roy Underhill's woodworking school. Schwarz was there, showing students how to build his anarchist's tool chest. Kuehn and Schwarz talked about how to improve a dovetail guide Kuehn owned. Schwarz dared him to make a better one. "That was enough for me." Kuehn says. "The gauntlet was thrown." His first batch of forty guides sold out in two days. By the end of the year, he had launched his toolmaking business.

Today, Schwarz divides his time between furniture commissions, his teaching and writing, and Lost Art Press, the publishing house he co-founded in 2007 with John Hoffman, another woodworker. The press maintains a storefront in Covington, Kentucky, where Schwarz and a roster of visiting craftspeople teach classes in chair making, spoon carving, and more.

He even has a small line of tools he sells under the Crucible name. "This is one of the odd things we do," he tells me. "There are tools that no one else will make, like our holdfast. So we found a foundry and now we make them. We were also trying to get manufacturers to make a good English lump hammer, but no one would. So we make them." The hammer is featured on page 160.

Frank Strazza

Austin, Texas

www.strazzafurniture.com

Frank Strazza admits that his Roubo benches "are a little over the top, but maybe they will inspire a woodworker to do good work."

Not only does Strazza mix light and dark woods, which make the large dovetails on the tail-vise chop stand out, but he also adorns his benches with inlays and marquetry. He uses Benchcrafted hardware.

Strazza came to woodworking early. "My first recollection was when my mom bought me an eggbeater-style drill," he says. "I was seven years old. At a fairly young age, I knew I wanted to work with my hands. I signed up for a class and cut my first dovetail when I was eleven. When I was twelve, I made a cedar chest that my parents still have at the foot of their bed."

He began an apprenticeship at age seventeen in a shop in Austin, Texas, making furniture from reclaimed wood. From there, he studied with Paul Sellers, a venerable British woodworker. Now in his forties, Strazza makes workbenches and custom furniture in a small shop that holds a large planer, an eight-inch jointer, two band saws, a drill press, and three benches. "Things are pretty tight," Strazza says. His custom period furniture has won numerous awards.

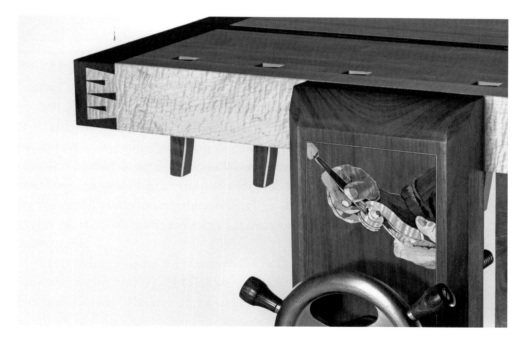

FACING PAGE, LEFT: Strazza calls the joint on his workbench's tail vise "hand-cut houndstooth dovetails."

FACING PAGE, RIGHT: Strazza (right) worked with client Sam Bright (left) to build this six-foot bench with a sapele base and a beech top.

TOP: Frank Strazza makes Roubo benches from carefully chosen woods and with elaborate marquetry, elevating an otherwise utilitarian object.

ABOVE: For a workbench for a violin maker, Strazza added a marquetry panel made of 120 pieces of wood to the walnut chop of the leg vise.

RE-CO BKLYN

Flushing, New York

www.recobklyn.com

RE-CO BKLYN salvages wood from the New York City area, selling it as the raw material for tabletops and other furniture, and as a Roubo workbench kit. The bench comes with four-by-six-inch legs; the tops are six inches thick, six to eleven feet long, and eighteen to twenty-three inches wide. A basic bench kit includes a chop for the leg vise, but no hardware. RE-CO recommends the screw and handle from Acer-Ferrous, Benchcrafted, or Lake Erie Toolworks.

The wood for the benches is red oak, which may be an endangered species in the area. As the company explains on its blog, "The fate of urban red oak trees once laying on their sides is grim. The problem is twofold. There are a lot of red oak trees in the New York metro area. Therefore, there are a lot of downed red oaks when storms roll through. Red oak holds only a fraction of the value that other species like black walnut and cherry do because of public perception and social trends. We happen to think that red oak is an extremely attractive wood and are doing our best to change that perception and show people how beautiful and unique red oak can be for furniture and other decor. These workbenches are an exciting opportunity to prove another use for this beautiful, versatile and strong as an ox material."

RE-CO BKLYN's specialty is salvaging red oak trees that have been toppled in storms and repurposing them as Roubo benches, which it sells either fully assembled or as a kit.

Old Wood, New Benches

Beginning in 2013, a few Roubo-bench enthusiasts have gathered regularly in Barnesville, Georgia, at Bo Childs's shop, to spend a week making new benches from old slabs of oak that Bo imports from France. This is the French Oak Roubo Project, or FORP, and it's certainly unique among group woodworking activities.

The wood for FORP is oak that has been air-drying for at least ten years. Jameel Abraham, of Benchcrafted, tells me more about the wood's history: "It's said that Thomas Jefferson brought American white oak seedlings to France and gifted them to Marie Antoinette. In the 1990s, a windstorm blew over some of the oaks that Antoinette planted at Versailles." A Benchcrafted blog post from 2013 declared, "There's a good chance these trees and Roubo were contemporaries. Roubo could have even touched one of these trees." (That's the sort of statement that ought to be true.)

The slabs are five to six inches thick, eighteen to twenty-eight inches wide, and about nineteen feet long. It takes three people to muscle one of those slabs around Childs's shop.

Childs has some pretty interesting machines, beginning with a Wood Mizer

Teamwork is the name of the game at the French Oak Roubo Project. It requires several hands to move a gargantuan slab over a jointer.

portable sawmill to cut the wood to rough length. Inside his shop is a vintage Oliver Machinery Straitoplane, which can flatten both sides of a slab in one pass. A Northlight Precision Straight Line Rip Saw uses a laser guide and an automatic feeder to quickly rip planks to width. And a Martin T12 spindle moulder can cut a one-by-two-inch tenon in one pass.

Even with all the horsepower, though, transforming the wood from rough timber to finished legs, stretchers, and tops requires plenty of human muscle—as you can see from the photos on these pages.

Participants built some twenty benches at the 2019 French Oak Roubo Project. Benchtops like the one shown here were cut from single pieces of aged white oak.

Lake Erie Toolworks

Erie, Pennsylvania
www.lakeerietoolworks.com

Lake Erie Toolworks uses hard maple for all the wooden tools it makes: vise-screw kits and Moxon vises. Nick and Jeff Dombrowski, a father-and-son team, started the business in 2008. Nick tells me, "We made a lot of expensive firewood until we got something salable" for the vise screws. It didn't hurt that his son, Jeff, was working for a company that makes and repairs pipe organs. Today, they work in a shop in Erie, Pennsylvania. They use a large CNC router with a custom rotary axis designed and built by Nick to turn the threads on the vise screws. They also make all the metal parts needed to hold the vise screws on a workbench.

The company introduced a line of solid maple traditional-style benches in early 2020. Called the ForeverBench, they are made with furniture-grade drawbored mortise-and-tenon joints. Lake Erie Toolworks also makes Moxon vise kits in two sizes, plus several kits for leg, shoulder, and tail vises.

Lake Erie Toolworks has branched out from making vise hardware to making a full-fledged workbench. It features drawbored joints, which hold the legs and stretchers together tightly.

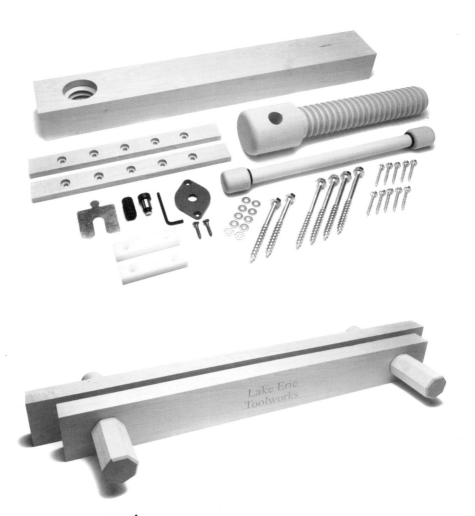

ABOVE: These parts are for a Lake Erie Toolworks leg vise. The company uses a customized CNC router to cut the threads on its vise screws.

LEFT: Nick Dombrowski handles much of the company's woodworking.

Acer-Ferrous Toolworks

Ridgefield, Pennsylvania

redrosereproductions.com

Acer-Ferrous Toolworks makes hard-maple wood screws and nuts for Moxon vises, leg vises, and adjustable stools. Paul Peters, the machinist behind Acer-Ferrous, tells me he was making a workbench a few years ago and wanted it to have a leg vise. When he saw an online ad for a screw, he knew he could make one himself. He began selling his leg vise in 2016, giving the product a formal introduction at a Lie-Nielsen event the following year. He sells his screws through Red Rose Reproductions (page 140). Peters says, "Business is going great. Two years ago, I decided to buckle down and build my inventory. I worked hard at that, but I still don't have an inventory. It goes out as fast as I can make it."

Acer-Ferrous's Paul Peters is a versatile machinist who makes not only wood screws and nuts for Moxon vises but also a measuring device called a sector, featured on page 65.

Texas Heritage Woodworks
Cedar Park, Texas
www.txheritage.net

Texas Heritage Woodworks is probably best known as a maker of shop aprons and tool rolls made with leather and waxed canvas. Jason Thigpen, the company's founder, decided to add Moxon-vise hardware made from ⅝-inch threaded rod and nuts. At first, he assembled the parts with a friend. "My friend would come over, we'd do some homebrew beer, and assemble the kits. But when I realized that the hardware wasn't something I could do continually, I reached out to Levi Green, a hot-rod fabricator. Now, I have one of the best street-rod builders making my hardware."

ABOVE: Jason Thigpen of Texas Heritage Woodworks makes a basic Moxon vise kit that uses thick threaded rods for the screws.

LEFT: Thigpen calls this long vise a chairmaker's vise. It's meant for holding a seat slab when shaping the sides.

Blum Tool Co.

Walnut, Iowa

blumtool.com

Gary Blum calls himself "an inveterate tinkerer" who started his tool-making business in 2007, while he was recovering from surgery. He lives and works in Walnut, Iowa, a small town west of Des Moines that straddles Interstate 80. Today, he makes innovative wood-bodied hand planes (see page 142), a unique sharpening jig, and decidedly un-Roubo workbenches.

"They don't look like much," he tells me. "I had one buyer who said he could make one in a morning—as he was ordering one of mine. Another person said he could make a bench very competitively in China." The heart of a Blum bench is a torsion box faced with ½-inch or ¾-inch plywood. (A torsion box is like a hollow-core door. It consists of a wood gridwork covered with a lightweight face. The resulting structure is light, strong, stiff, and flat.) Pipe clamps comprise the vise hardware on a Blum bench. Blum's stationary benches have wood legs; his portable benches use detachable or folding metal legs. A row of holes along the front of a Blum bench allows the vise assembly to be repositioned anywhere along the length of the bench. •

Blum developed a love of vintage tools when he was a student at Iowa State University, in the mid-1970s. "My girlfriend requested that I make something for her. That's when I started buying tools. I had a love of tools and old tools very early on. I'd go to flea markets and old-time hardware stores in Des Moines and Omaha and seek out tools and keep them in my dresser. I was making furniture by hand in my dorm room."

He majored in vocational agriculture and spent two years teaching the subject, then decided to go into furniture making and cabinetmaking instead. He keeps that business going alongside the toolmaking.

In a way, Blum's portable benches hark back to his college days, when his dorm room doubled as a woodshop. He says hobbyists and people living in apartments are the biggest customers for his small benches. Blum Tool's cabinetmakers benches range from seventy-two to ninety inches long. Blum also sells tops and vises without a base.

ABOVE: Blum Tool Co.'s cabinetmaker's bench comes in lengths from seventy-two to ninety inches. The holes in the sides allow users to reposition the pipe-clamp vises.

LEFT: Blum's maker's bench is meant for people who have a small shop. Tops on this model range from forty-eight to sixty-six inches in length.

BELOW: Gary Blum began woodworking in college and still has a cabinetmaking business, which he runs alongside his tool company.

The Japanese Approach

Workbenches in the United States and Europe share one trait: they are designed to immobilize wood through the use of vises, holdfasts, and bench dogs. The benches are massive and heavy, with enough bulk to keep everything steady.

Woodworkers who practice Japanese techniques have a totally different take on the workbench. To learn more about this, I visited Andrew Hunter at his home and shop in New York's Hudson Valley.

Hunter has spent the past twenty years making beautifully proportioned, practical furniture using Japanese methods and hand tools. He is a frequent contributor to *Fine Woodworking* magazine and often exhibits at woodworking shows, where he demonstrates his prowess with Japanese hand planes by pulling impossibly thin shavings from a thick piece of cherry.

To Western eyes, Hunter's workbench might look like a work in progress. Three thick slabs of poplar, each seven feet long, rest on a pair of sturdy trestles made of hemlock—at first glance, not much different from any other bench. But this Japanese-style bench is not meant to immobilize wood so much as to position it for planing and sawing. The bench, the work, and the woodworker act together as a system to keep things steady.

The poplar slabs are purposely left loose on the trestles. That way, Hunter can move them apart or tilt one on edge to make room for clamps. One slab has holes drilled along the length for wood pegs that serve as a stop for a workpiece and as a brace to anchor the slab to a trestle. To fix a peg tightly in a hole, Hunter wraps a stray plane shaving around it. If Hunter has a job that requires him to work at a client's site, he can easily transport the slabs and trestles in his minivan.

Hunter tells me he flattened the poplar slabs when he made the bench twenty years ago. They remain flat today. His bench is usually as steady as any other. Any movement is a warning sign. "If things are moving around on the bench, then I know my tools aren't sharp enough," he told me.

When Hunter needs to saw at the bench, he positions the wood against a couple of pegs, holds the wood with his free hand, and kneels down so he has the workpiece at eye level. "If I'm cutting dovetails," he says, "this position lets me see the top, front, and bottom of the piece I will be sawing."

Hunter also has a pair of sawhorses, each less than a foot high. When he wants to rip a board, he props one end against a sawhorse, steadies it with one foot, and leans over to make the cut. He will also sit on the floor, with the wood straddling both sawhorses, for other cutting. "Sitting on the floor is ideal," he says. "Then the whole world is my workbench."

TOP: Andrew Hunter's Japanese-style workbench consists of thick poplar planks resting loosely on a pair of trestles. The holes in one plank hold pegs for steadying the work.

ABOVE: Razor-sharp tools minimize the need to clamp work on the bench. If things begin to move, Hunter says, "I know my tools aren't sharp enough."

RIGHT: A pair of low trestles make perfectly functional sawhorses. Hunter can also sit on the floor and work at trestle height.

Squares, Gauges,
Marking Knives, and Awls

AFTER A GOOD WORKBENCH, good measuring and marking tools are must-haves for woodworkers. That's because everything you do in the shop begins with a measurement of some kind, and you want your measurements to be both accurate and repeatable. Achieving those ends requires a small arsenal of tools.

The combination square is arguably the most versatile, as you can use it to mark angles at forty-five and ninety degrees. You can also use it to strike a line parallel to the edge, by holding a pencil against the end of the blade as you slide the head along the board. And you can remove the head and use it to check the alignment of a table-saw or band-saw blade or a jointer fence.

A double square and a try square handle many of the same functions as a combination square, but only for right angles. (There are try squares with a blade set at forty-five degrees, for miters.) A double square has a sliding head, while the head of a try square is pinned to the blade. All these squares come in sizes ranging from two inches up to twelve inches.

A carpenter's square is actually a triangle with a fence on one leg to register against a board. (This type of tool is also known as a speed square, a name coined by Swanson Tools, which invented it.) You can use the edges of the square to mark forty-five- and ninety-degree lines across a board. Holes and graduated lines on the edges of the square make it easy to scribe lines or find an angle.

For mortises and tenons, you'll need a mortising gauge and marking gauge. A marking gauge uses a sharp pin, a small knife blade, or a small, sharp wheel to scribe the wood to mark the length of a tenon or the depth of a dovetail joint. A mortising gauge is similar, but has two pins to outline the width of a mortise and the tenon it mates with. Many woodworkers keep several mortising and marking gauges on hand, using each one for a different measurement to avoid resetting the gauge and introducing the possibility of an error.

For dovetail joints, you want to use either a bevel gauge or a dedicated dovetail gauge, in conjunction with a marking knife and a marking gauge, to mark the depth of the joint and the angles for the pins and

Tools for measuring and marking include (from the left) a speed square, an adjustable double square, a try square, an awl, a combination square, a marking gauge, a bevel gauge—and, of course, a good sharp pencil.

tails. A marking knife gets into corners better than a pencil; in addition, a knife line is thinner than a pencil line and creates a shallow groove where you can position a chisel.

Marking knives have a blade ground flat on one side and beveled on the other. Some are just a plain piece of steel, while others have the blade set into a handle made from an exotic hardwood.

Finally, you need at least one awl. An awl is a very handy tool. I use mine most often to mark a center point on a hunk of wood that I'll shape into a bowl on the lathe. Once in a while, I'll use it to scribe a line on a piece of wood or make the pilot hole for a small screw.

The makers profiled in this chapter distinguish their products from mass-produced alternatives by using sumptuous materials and machining the metal to an almost insane level of accuracy. Although you may want to cradle these tools in your hands, they're meant to be put to work, not put on display.

Colen Clenton

Hunter Valley, New South Wales, Australia
www.instagram.com/colenclenton

Some thirty years ago, as a young woodworker, Colen Clenton learned two important lessons: squares aren't always square, and most can't be wrangled back into squareness. At the time, Clenton was in charge of jointing wood in a shop. "I would joint a piece of timber, but I couldn't get it crisp," he tells me. "I found that the inside and outside of the square weren't the same. They were out by about ten thousandths of an inch." (That's about ¹⁄₆₄ inch.) "I spent about two weeks' wages on an engineering square, and I thought that would do the trick," he says. "But as I walked out of the shop, the square slipped and landed on the concrete, right on the end of the blade."

What Clenton calls "my five minutes of fame" was his design for a square that can be adjusted. Then, as now, the body of most squares is held in place over the blade with several pins. Clenton's square has one pin to hold the parts together and two small screws that can be turned to push the blade one direction or another to true it to the body. He also makes similarly adjustable dovetail gauges, forty-five-degree markers, and T-squares.

Clenton began making tools (a cutting gauge was his first), and friends started asking him to make one for them. "After about five years of doing this, I realized there was a market for my tools," he says. He built his business through word of mouth and says it has been many years since he felt the need to advertise. Alone among the toolmakers I've interviewed, Clenton has no website, just a small Instagram account.

He currently lives in a wine-making region north of Sydney, working alone in a shop about the size of a three-car garage. Inside, Clenton has all the basic woodworking tools, plus a jointer, a band saw, a couple of planers, five grinders ("one for each grit because I hate changing belts"), a milling machine, and three metalworking lathes. He built a horizontal drill press to make holes in end grain for the adjusting screws. "I take little bites and get the holes spot on every time."

TOP: Colen Clenton produces try squares in sizes ranging from two to ten inches. They combine brass with rose she-oak or ebony.

ABOVE LEFT: Two small set screws in the base of a Clenton square allow you to adjust the blade if it should slip out of alignment.

ABOVE RIGHT: Clenton needs about two and a half hours to make a single square, but he works in batches, making dozens at a time.

To make a square, Clenton first dresses the wood, does all the grinding and lapping of the brass parts, and assembles it. A square takes him about two and a half hours, and he works in big batches. "The last time I did squares, I made about six hundred handles," he tells me.

His work isn't about speed or quantity, though. "I get up in the morning, come out to the shop, and do what I love doing," he says. "The ebony I use may come from a three-thousand-year-old tree. If you have any respect for the tree, then you should make something that will last at least as long as it took to grow the tree in the first place."

Clenton says orders by phone or email give him a welcome opportunity to chat with customers. In Australia, the plane-making company HNT Gordon & Co. (hntgordon.com.au) sells Clenton's squares, gauges, and awl. In the United States, Tools for Working Wood (toolsforworkingwood.com) sells the squares, the dovetail gauges, and various mortise and marking gauges.

LEFT: Clenton's angle gauges, for striking accurate miters, are also adjustable if they go out of alignment.

RIGHT: Clenton works alone and has a minimal presence on the internet. He enjoys taking phone orders, though, for they give him a chance to chat with his customers.

The Sector

Some of us are old enough to remember the slide rule—a tool with a sliding central bar and marked with logarithmic scales—to do all sorts of mathematical calculations. (Personally, I never got past the basic scale for multiplication, and the results I got were usually dodgy.) Electronic calculators and computers killed the slide rule, just as other advancements made other vintage measuring and calculating devices obsolete. Today, however, two people have brought back one of those devices—the sector.

A sector consists of two arms joined with a hinge and marked with two to four scales. The noted astronomer Galileo Galilei is generally credited with inventing the sector in the late 1500s. It's meant to be used in conjunction with dividers to divide a board into equal segments, to divide a circle into equal segments to create a polygon, to find an angle, or to find the radius, diameter, or circumference of a circle. You set the dividers to a known distance (the width of a board, say) and open the sector so you can fit the points of the dividers at the endpoints of the appropriate scale.

Then you reset the dividers to the point you want on that scale. For example, to divide that board into five segments, for laying out dovetails, you'd move the dividers to the 5-point and step off that distance across the board.

Acer-Ferrous Toolworks (page 54) makes a dandy sector with a brass hinge and aluminum arms. There are two scales etched into each side of the arms, along with registration points for the dividers. It also comes with a well-written instruction manual. It's available through Red Rose Reproductions (redrosereproductions.com).

Brendan Gaffney (www.burn-heart.com), a graduate of the Krenov School, conducts classes in the use of the sector. He made a batch of them in hard maple a few years ago. Although he doesn't use a sector much in his own woodworking, he says that understanding the sector "is a jumping-off point for the underlying geometry in woodworking."

Paul Peters, of Acer-Ferrous Toolworks, produces a gauge known as a sector. Developed during the Renaissance, it is used to divide a board, find the radius of a circle, and more.

Vesper Tools

Carrum Downs, Victoria, Australia

www.vespertools.com.au

Chris Vesper is perhaps best known for his sliding bevels and try squares with infills of exotic wood. "There's no gap between the brass and the infill," he says. "I make the infills in the milling machine. It's quite hard, so I do one run every year. I have a tolerance for the pocket and the infill of plus or minus half a thousandth. If the pocket is at the lower end of its tolerance and the infill is at the higher end, then I get a nice tight fit."

Vesper tells me, "There are six pins in a square—five to hold the blade and one to hold the tab. I make those pins in house, cutting and deburring round bar. They're small and fiddly. But most repetition machining I get done outside—things like brass knobs and other bits. There's no point to me standing at a manual lathe to do production work. It's not the right equipment for that, given the time and costs involved."

Vesper also makes a line of double squares based on old ones for tool and die makers. They have a precise forty-five-degree angle machined into one corner of the body and come with different blades: a thick one for general layout work and thinner ones for dovetails, machine setup, and depth measuring. A line of bevel gauges and marking knives rounds out his tools.

Vesper began making tools as a teenager in the mid-1990s because he couldn't afford to buy what he needed for his woodworking hobby. From 1998 onward, he sold small quantities of tools as a hobby. In 2003, he decided to be a full-time toolmaker. At first, he worked in a large pole barn he built on his parents' property. In 2016, he moved to a larger shop in an industrial area in the Melbourne suburbs.

He tells me, "When I was much younger, I might have said, 'I don't want to do this production stuff. I want to do my one-offs and special work.' But I came to learn that good production work is actually harder. You have to do something again and again and get the same level of finish and perfection. If I make a mistake or forget a step, I have to go back and do all that work over again to every part. It might only be a small batch of fifty or a hundred items, but it hurts to rework that. To do what I do, there are no magic shortcuts. The tools really are handmade."

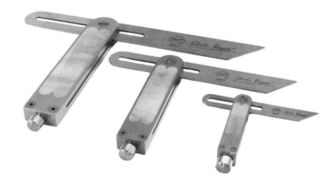

FACING PAGE: Chris Vesper's squares have a small spring-loaded tab on the handle, which helps keep the tool in position on a workpiece.

ABOVE LEFT: Vesper's double squares come with a conventional wide blade as well as a narrow blade, shown here, for work in tight quarters.

ABOVE RIGHT: The wood infill in Vesper's bevel gauges fits precisely in the brass housing, with no gaps.

LEFT: Vesper began making tools as a teenager and has seen his business grow steadily over the years. He now works from a two-story factory near Melbourne.

Blue Spruce Toolworks

Portland, Oregon
bluesprucetoolworks.com

Dave Jeske, the founder of Blue Spruce Toolworks, traded a career engineering things like submarine missile systems and portable milling machines for life as a hand-tool maker.

After college, he rekindled an interest in woodworking that he had in his youth. When he couldn't find a good marking knife for laying out dovetails, he made one. He posted images of his knife on Neanderthal Haven, an early internet forum, and began selling. "I was doing this on the side so I could make money to buy vintage tools," he says.

Jeske met John Economaki, founder of Bridge City Tool Works (page 25) through the forum. For several years, he made marking knives, chisels, and other tools for Economaki's company. Jeske continued toolmaking under the Blue Spruce banner. He now has a line of try squares, bevel gauges, and miter squares akin to Colen Clenton's tools. The Blue Spruce squares have an aluminum body with hardwood infill and two adjusting screws. His extensive line of marking knives includes a mix-and-match set of knives, scribes, and three awls. You can choose from one of four handles, four collets, and nine blades to complete the set. "I thought people might want a different knife for different purposes," he says, so he decided to make one knife and different blades rather than a bunch of knives.

In 2019, Jeske sold Blue Spruce to Woodpeckers (page 30). When I asked if this meant he'd have to begin using Woodpeckers's signature red aluminum in his work, he laughed and said no. "I'll do prototype work to produce in Ohio," he says, referring to Woodpeckers's location. "One thing I like most about toolmaking is being able to bring a new product to market. I like the design work and figuring out how to get it made."

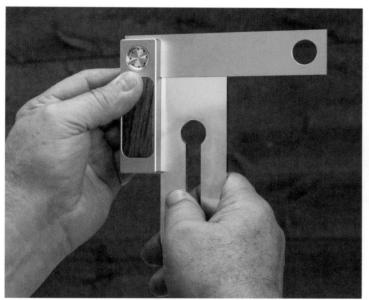

CLOCKWISE FROM TOP LEFT: Blue Spruce offers a unique marking set, with three handles that accept various marking knife blades and awls. The company offers mix-and-match choices for its bevel gauges—seven colors of anodized aluminum for the body and three woods for the infill. Blue Spruce founder Dave Jeske began selling his tools on an early internet forum. Blue Spruce squares have adjusting screws, like those from Colen Clenton, to keep them in alignment. A batch of miter-square bodies ready to be fitted with hardwood infill.

Bridge City Tool Works

see page 25

—

Bridge City has an innovative multipurpose layout and setup tool that combines a protractor, a bevel gauge, a try square, a dovetail gauge, a depth gauge, a marking gauge, and a centering rule. You can use the tool to lay out mortise-and-tenon or dovetail joints, check the depth of the mortise, or set the tilt of a table-saw blade or the saw's miter fence. You can also use the tool to set the tilt on a drill-press table. The accuracy of the tool's fixed square is plus or minus two thousandths over the length of the 3 ½-inch leg.

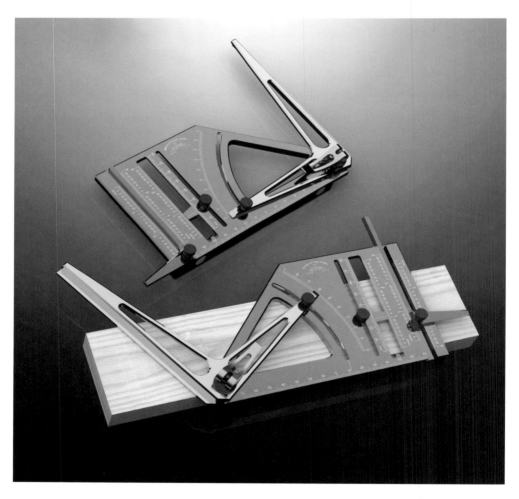

Many products from Bridge City Tool Works are multifunctional—perhaps none more so than this seven-function, extremely accurate layout and marking tool.

Sterling Tool Works

see page 162

Sterling makes the Dovetail Square, a unique double square that's especially helpful for making dovetails. You can order the square with both a graduated ruler and an ungraduated blade designed to check the squareness of a joint. The ungraduated Dovetail Blade has a narrow end and a wide end so you can reach into places that are too narrow for a conventional square.

The Sterling Tool Works Dovetail Square comes with a thin, ungraduated blade that's designed to reach into narrow spaces (above right) or a conventional graduated blade (right).

Shenandoah Tool Works

see page 161

Shenandoah also makes a birdcage awl, using 01 tool steel that's twisted along most of its length. The handles, individually turned from highly figured hardwoods, have a shape that fits the hand comfortably.

A birdcage awl was once actually used to make birdcages. Today, it's a sturdy tool for marking center points and starter holes.

Blackburn Tools

see page 100

Blackburn Tools has what the saw maker Isaac Smith terms a "scrawl," with a long handle like that on a marking knife.

Blackburn Tools mainly makes hand-saw kits. But it also produces this long-handled awl that it calls a scrawl.

Glen-Drake Toolworks

Fort Bragg, California
www.glen-drake.com

Kevin Glen Drake got his start as a toolmaker in the early 2000s with a brass marking gauge. The one he had been using infuriated him. "It was too hard to adjust. It was finicky." He threw it into the street. He designed his own version of a micro-adjustable gauge he had seen in Jim Klingshott's book *Making and Modifying Woodworking Tools*. He had a few gauges made and sold them to students at his alma mater, the College of the Redwoods.

He also sent one to Thomas Lie-Nielsen (page 14), who immediately placed an order. Drake says that he would not be in business if it were not for Lie-Nielsen, who "sets the standard for quality woodworking tools." Today, Drake sells his Tite-Mark gauge on his website and through Lie-Nielsen as well as other toolmakers and retailers worldwide.

Drake works closely with a local machine shop to fabricate the parts, which he assembles and tunes in his shop. He says, "You will find my fingerprints on every tool that goes out the door." He works to a tolerance of two-tenths of a thousandth. "I'm pretty addicted to precision," he says.

Users can add accessories to the basic Tite-Mark for scoring, paring, and precision layout of mortises and tenons. "People are constantly finding uses for the Tite-Mark that I never imagined," Drake says. "I find that to be very gratifying."

Drake says, "I've always been a tool freak. I was a musician for close to twenty years in the Los Angeles area, and I spent almost as much time playing with the instruments as I did playing music. When I took up woodworking, I went pretty nuts over the tools." When he was in his mid-fifties, he studied woodworking at the school founded by James Krenov in Fort Bragg, California. He stayed in town after graduation and set up his shop in 2001. Ron Hock, the plane-blade maker extraordinaire (page 139), is around the corner.

ABOVE: The Tite-Mark gauge is meant to be used with one hand and can be outfitted with a single wheel for scoring a line or adjustable double wheels for outlining a mortise.

LEFT: Kevin Glen Drake, developer of the Tite-Mark, studied woodworking with James Krenov and periodically returns to Krenov's school to talk about hand saws.

Florip Toolworks

see page 92

—

Florip sells a gauge that resembles the Glen-Drake Toolworks Tite-Mark, but only at first glance. "They're both adjustable-wheel marking gauges made from brass," Erik Florip says. "Their method of function is different. I put in an effort to make sure I wasn't pulling Drake's design."

Florip's gauge uses an enclosed collar to hold the knurled portion of the gauge. When you turn that portion, only the fence moves. Drake's gauge has a left-hand thread at the bottom and a right-hand thread at the top. When you turn the adjustment portion, it moves with the fence.

Florip's basic gauge also has a flat ground into the fence; his larger gauge has a six-sided fence. Those features prevent the gauge from rolling off the bench. The basic gauge can also strike a line on ⅛-inch-thick material while being supported on the work surface.

Erik Florip designed his marking gauges to stay put on the bench. The larger gauge, shown here, has a hexagonal face. The smaller model has a flat ground into the face.

Hamilton Toolworks
Springdale, Arkansas
www.hamiltontools.com

Several companies make a marking knife that consists of a spear-point blade attached to a turned handle of exotic hardwood. These knives are all well made, but hardly unique. Jeff Hamilton's Hamilton Toolworks makes a knife that stands apart from the pack. It has a flat hardwood handle and a wood sheath to protect the blade.

"I got tired of using a knife with a round handle, because every time I used it I knocked it on the floor," he tells me. So he spent two years making prototypes and showing them to friends. He began selling the knife in December 2018. "The first batch of knives lasted about two minutes," he says.

Hamilton also makes a line of wood-bodied marking gauges. He began making them after taking a class at the Marc Adams School of Woodworking in Indiana. "The Japanese-style marking gauge I was using was so big that I couldn't lay out the joints," he says. He made his own and showed it to Marc Adams, who connected him with another student who agreed to sell Hamilton's gauges. For the next couple of years, he sold twenty-five to thirty gauges a year. Then he attended a Woodworking in America conference, where he got some suggestions for improvements from Dave Jeske of Blue Spruce Toolworks. After that, he says, "the business went from twenty-five a year to twenty-five a week."

Jeff Hamilton's marking knife has a flat handle and a wood sheath for the blade. He sized the heads on his marking gauges so they wouldn't interfere with the work.

DFM Tool Works
Chicago, Illinois
dfmtoolworks.com

DFM Tool Works makes a line of marking knives as well as aluminum squares. The company offers six knives, all without handles and with different blade configurations: left-hand and right-hand, symmetrical or asymmetrical bevel.

One small square that DFM makes is an L-shaped piece of aluminum with large holes along the legs. The holes hold pins that allow the square to be used as a center finder, for scribing a line along the length of a board. The other, a carpenter's square, has scribing notches every 1/16 inch, as well as guides for common rafter angles and slots for laying out polygons.

RIGHT: DFM Tool Works sells different styles of marking-knife blades. The holes in the metal are for rivets you use to attach your own wood handles.

BELOW LEFT: DFM's version of the venerable speed square is filled with gauges and spaces for a pencil, so you can use the square to strike lines.

BELOW RIGHT: The movable pins in this small square from DFM are meant to straddle a board, so you can put a pencil in the hole between the pins to mark a centerline.

Seth Gould

Bakersville, North Carolina

www.sethgould.com

Seth Gould was a resident artist at North Carolina's Penland School of Craft from 2015 to 2018 and is still closely associated with the school. He earned a degree in jewelry design and fine metalworking, and now makes functional tools and objets d'art. His dividers and outside calipers are all business. He produces tools in small batches and begins production when he gets enough names on a waiting list.

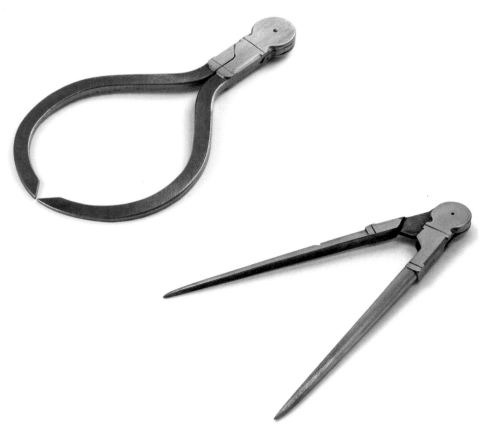

Seth Gould makes refined versions of utilitarian tools, including the calipers shown above and the dividers shown at the right.

Czeck Edge Hand Tool

Marietta, Georgia
www.czeckedge.com

The birdcage awl originally had a much different purpose than a standard awl. Robert Zajicek of Czeck Edge Hand Tool makes this type of awl. As he explains, "A birdcage awl was used centuries ago to make birdcages. You'd take these thin strips of wood, bore holes in them with the awl, and insert reeds in the holes to assemble a birdcage." Accordingly, the shaft of a birdcage awl is about ¼-inch square, ground to a pyramidal point at the end.

The awls from Czeck Edge are made of either carbon steel or carbide. Zajicek calls carbide indestructible. "You won't ever have to sharpen it," he says. "Even your grandchildren won't have to sharpen it." Zajicek should know. His company was the first to use carbide in hand tools, beginning with its Kerf Kadet marking knife.

Zajicek began toolmaking in 2005, after retiring from a career in aerospace. He picked up an interest in woodworking as a child. "Instead of getting cap guns, we got hammers and nails," he told me. "My dad never had the inclination to buy nails in a box. We would go to construction sites, find crappy wood, bang out the nails and straighten them on the sidewalk."

In addition to the awls and marking knife, Zajicek makes a unique ruler stop, which allows a ruler or straightedge to function as a square. He also sells the awls and marking knife in kit form.

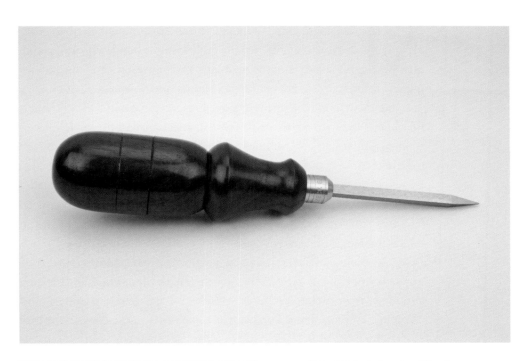

ABOVE: Robert Zajicek, founder of Czeck Edge Hand Tool, makes the shaft of his birdcage awl from carbide. "It's indestructible," he says. "You won't ever have to sharpen it."

LEFT: Zajicek developed a lifelong love of woodworking from his father. He founded his tool business after retiring from a career in aerospace.

Hand Saws

MANY WOODWORKERS TODAY seldom pick up a hand saw. Instead, they fire up the table saw, the band saw, or the chop saw to rip boards to width, crosscut them to length, slice pieces of veneer, or cut curves, tapers, tenons, and dovetails.

But until the invention of the powered circular saw in the early 1800s, hand saws handled all those functions, and handled them well. Over time, woodworkers and toolmakers developed a range of saws optimized for different tasks. Workers wielded large, heavy, two-man saws (also known as pit saws) to reduce logs to rough-dimensioned boards. Smaller versions of those saws, called frame saws, were used to cut veneers. Ripsaws and crosscut saws did the everyday work of cutting wood to width and length. Instead of those tools, some woodworkers used a variant of the frame saw known as a bow saw. Joiners and cabinetmakers used fine-toothed saws of various sizes, with a thick piece of brass stiffening (backing) the blade, to do the fine work of shaping tenons, miters, and dovetails. You could find a similar tool, known as a gent's saw, in the tool chest of many an upper-crust dilettante in the nineteenth century.

The types of saws developed in the eighteenth and nineteenth centuries are still in use today, many of them made in one- and two-person shops with devoted followers. (Japanese saws are different from Western saws in nearly every way, as the sidebar on page 86 explains.)

These saw makers speak a very specialized vocabulary. The metal part with teeth is properly termed the *plate*. It's often ground to be thinner at the top, so the saw doesn't bind in the cut. The wood handle is known as the *tote*. And there are several terms to describe the geometry of the teeth. On most saws, the teeth are *set*, or bent alternately left and right to prevent the plate from binding. *Rake* defines the angle of the front of each tooth. *Fleam* (a word from the Middle Ages that's also associated with bloodletting) defines the bevel angle filed on the front of each tooth. *Slope* defines the bevel filed on the trailing edge of the teeth; a crosscut saw optimized for cutting softwoods will have a steeper slope than one optimized for hardwoods or for ripping. *Pitch* refers to the number of points or teeth per inch; most saws have a uniform pitch, but some

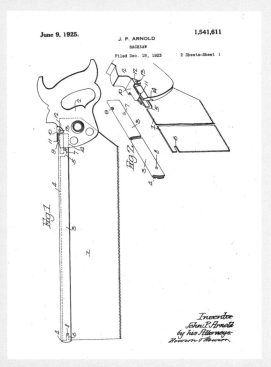

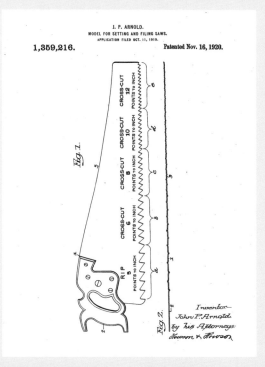

Patent drawings from the early twentieth century reflect the continual interest among inventors and toolmakers to improve on centuries-old designs. Present-day saw makers continue to look for ways to improve tools or make them with greater precision.

feature progressive pitch, with the number of teeth per inch changing along the length of the plate. *Breasting* defines a saw plate with a gently curved edge for the teeth; one theory has it that breasting helps keep the saw centered in the cut. Not all saws are breasted. Finally, *hang* refers to the angle of the tote in relation to the blade. Ideally, the hang of a saw will put your forearm and wrist in line with the saw teeth, so you can keep your arm straight as you cut.

Disston and Sons was by far the world's leading maker of hand saws in the late nineteenth and early twentieth centuries. Disston designs are still the touchstone for many modern-day hand-saw makers, who copy the shape of the plate, the shape of the tote, or both. Other makers emulate traditional English designs for backsaws. The norms for modern saw makers are totes shaped from exotic hardwoods, high-quality steel for the plate, and razor-sharp teeth.

Skelton Saws
Scarborough, North Yorkshire, England
www.skeltonsaws.co.uk

Shane Skelton, a young saw maker in Scarborough, England, is matter-of-factly immodest. "I am the only person in the world making saws of this quality," he declares. "We are in the saw world what Karl Holtey is in hand planes." (See page 106 for Holtey Classic Hand Planes.)

Working from his garage, Skelton makes a range of saws based on Georgian designs. "Our style is based on the eighteenth century, when one or two people worked in a saw shop. The saws were essentially bespoke, and you could tell which shop made the saw. What happened after the eighteenth century was that companies worked faster. The little saw makers all disappeared. In Sheffield, within a few years the saws all looked identical. We've shifted right back to when saws were individually made."

Shane Skelton gives each of his saw designs
a backstory. The Swift dovetail saw, shown here,
takes its name from the Supermarine Swift,
an early jet fighter plane with swept-back wings.

ABOVE: Working in a small shop in Yorkshire, England, Skelton makes only about eight saws a month. He likens his tools to custom-made Savile Row suits.

LEFT: Shaping a batch of handles, or totes, takes Skelton about two weeks. He makes all the parts for his saws, including the fasteners that hold plate and tote together.

Skelton's wife, Jaq, is also his business partner.
Among many other things, she researches the
backstory for each of the saws.

Skelton does all the manufacturing. "There's nothing in the tool that was not made by my hand," he says. Working alone, he makes eight saws a month, on average. He spends about two weeks on the woodwork, a similar amount of time on the metalwork. He cuts saw plates to size, grinds a taper by hand, and hammers the steel to tension it. He uses a small fly press to stamp out the teeth one at a time and sets the teeth by hand. Similarly, he uses hand planes, files, and rasps to produce the totes. He has a small metalworking lathe to turn out bolts, medallions, and other hardware. He and his wife, Jaq, even mix their own oil-and-wax wood finish, which they call Skelton Saws Peacock Oil. "My saws are like made-to-measure Savile Row suits," he says. His craftsmanship is impeccable. Wait times for a Skelton saw range from eight months to a year.

Skelton learned metalworking first, beginning with a part-time job with a blacksmith while he was a student. Later, he worked for a gunsmith, where he learned how to handle metalworking machinery. He also worked for a cabinetmaker and furniture restorer, where he specialized in refurbishing fine pieces from the eighteenth century. "I found that I couldn't buy a saw that would cut straight the way I wanted. So I decided

Skelton's Chippendale dovetail saw is an homage to the famous furniture maker. Skelton studied the dovetails of a famous Chippendale piece to determine the proper set for the saw teeth.

to have a go at making saws," he tells me. He sent one of his first saws to David Charlesworth, a highly respected English furniture maker and teacher. At the time, he said to himself, "If he likes it, I know I'm going down the right path." Charlesworth loved the saw.

Jaq Skelton, a former teacher, set up the business two months after she laid eyes on Skelton's first saw, and she remains an equal and indispensable part of the enterprise. Among many other things, she does the historical research needed to give all the saws a backstory. For example, their Swift dovetail saw has a curved nose that, Shane says, was inspired by an early British fighter jet with swept-back wings like the feathered swift. His gent's saw, the Gentleman Jaq, is named for two astute businesswomen— his wife and the title character in a BBC series, *Gentleman Jack*. And his Chippendale line pays homage to the cabinetmaker and features an innovative dual-spring mechanism to keep the blade properly tensioned.

A Few Words about Japanese Saws

Japanese hand saws are different from their Western counterparts in some important ways. They have a straight handle, not a tote. Some come with cross-cut teeth on one edge, rip teeth on the opposite edge. They use replaceable plates, so they don't need sharpening. Most importantly, they're the only saws in the world that cut on the pull stroke. It's not known for certain why that's the case, but the noted woodworker Toshio Ōdate has a plausible explanation in his book *Japanese Woodworking Tools*:

"In ancient Japan, *shokunin* [artisans] typically worked in a squatting or sitting position; even today, many craftsmen work seated on a mat on the floor. If you try to push a saw in a sitting position, you cannot use your body weight and arm muscles for power. The opposite stroke—pulling—is far better, for you can use the muscles of your entire body to make the cut."

In addition, cutting on the pull stroke puts the saw plate in tension, so it's less likely to bind. This also means the plate can be thinner than that on a Western-style saw. Because of these characteristics, a Japanese saw cuts a very thin kerf. The most common type of Japanese saw is known as *ryoba noko*, which simply means "double-edged saw." The *azebiki nokogiri* is a type of *ryoba* saw with an extremely short, breasted plate. It's used to begin a cut in the middle of a board and to cut curves. A single-edged saw is called a *kataba*. A *kataba*-style *azebiki nokogiri* is often used to cut long, deep grooves. A *dozuki* saw is essentially a *kataba* with a steel or brass back on a very thin plate. It takes its name from the tenon shoulders (*dozuki*) it cuts.

Four of the companies profiled in this book—Lee Valley (page 20), Bridge City Tool Works (page 25), Woodpeckers (page 30), and Tools for Working Wood (page 96)—sell Japanese pull saws.

I bought my first Japanese saw in the mid-1980s, when I needed some tools to renovate the apartment my wife and I had just purchased. The benefits of cutting on the pull stroke became crystal-clear the first time I used the saw. I've never used another type of saw since.

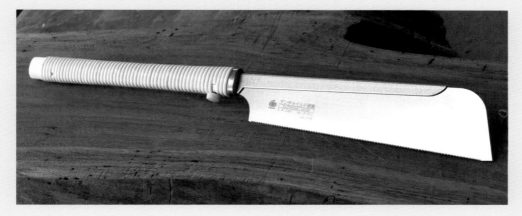

TOP: A *kataba*, or single-edged Japanese saw.

CENTER: A *ryoba noko*, or double-edged saw, with crosscut teeth on one side and rip teeth on the other.

BOTTOM: A *dozuki*, a backed saw for cutting tenons or dovetails.

Bad Axe Tool Works

Superior, Wisconsin
www.badaxetoolworks.com

Mark Harrell, the founder of Bad Axe Tool Works, learned to sharpen saws before deciding to make them. In the early 2000s, he tells me, he had retired as a colonel after a twenty-eight-year career in the US Army and "wanted to do something with an entrepreneurial bent." He had already developed a strong interest in timber framing, saying, "Twenty years ago, I built my own cabin off the grid—and that's when I fell in love with old tools and what made them sing." He began buying timber-framing tools, then other hand tools. Like many others, he progressed from tool buyer to tool restorer to toolmaker.

"I was determined to learn how to sharpen my own hand saw," he says. "Along the way, I butchered three or four old saws. But then I got a thirty-inch Millers Falls miter saw, and it all came together one night shortly after my retirement. That's when I realized, if I can do this, then I can market this skill."

In 2008, he developed a following on eBay by selling old saws that he restored and sharpened. By 2009, he decided to begin making saws from scratch.

Harrell named his company for Wisconsin's Bad Axe River. The name is in honor of Black Hawk, chief of the Fox/Sauk Indians, who fought for land around the river during an 1832 war with Andrew Jackson. The Bad Axe River also happens to be where Harrell had built his cabin.

Today, he and Bad Axe co-owner Yvonne L'Abbe, Harrell's wife, operate their saw-making enterprise from a three-thousand-square-foot shop in Superior, Wisconsin. He and his crew duplicate and improve upon old designs, notably vintage Disston and Sons saws.

Bad Axe obtains saw-plate steel from mills in the United States, Sweden, Austria, and Germany. Suppliers in the United States provide totes, fasteners, and sawbacks based on designs Harrell developed that are true to components from the late 1800s. The Bad Axe crew establishes the tooth line, sets and sharpens the teeth, and assembles the saws. Harrell explains, "We leave handle, sawback, and fastener fabrication to professionals with state-of-the-art equipment, giving us the freedom and

ABOVE: Bad Axe Tool Works makes a wide range of hand saws, from small ones meant for cutting grooves for the frets on a guitar to big ones meant to rip boards to width.

LEFT: The teeth on Bad Axe saws are set individually with a fixture called a hammer set, which cleanly creases the tooth.

TOP: The saw teeth are filed by hand at Bad Axe. It's a procedure that looks tedious, but saw makers swear it's quick and easy.

ABOVE: A close-up view of a hammer set, essentially a spring-loaded anvil activated with a hammer blow.

RIGHT: Bad Axe founder Mark Harrell set up the company after a few years of restoring antique saws and selling them online.

time to do what we do best: creating a dead-nuts precise tooth line based on an incredibly consistent set and expertly sharpened teeth."

Bad Axe uses hammer sets to set the teeth on its saws. Rather than bending the teeth, the hammer set strikes a tooth against a beveled anvil, creating a clean crease above the gullet. It's a procedure that metalworkers call coining. "Saw steel is a spring steel alloy and doesn't want to cooperate," Harrell says (in a nod to his army days). "Am I going to get my way by squeezing each tooth into place with a plier set, or by smacking the tooth into a precise set, like a drill sergeant getting troops into formation?" The Bad Axe crew uses digital calipers to refine that set, based on the thickness of the plate and the type of saw they're making.

Several years ago, Harrell moved away from brass, bronze, and copper sawbacks to black-oxide steel sawbacks or steel plated with titanium nitride, a coating that resembles bronze. "I can't stand brass," he says. "It's a weak metal and does not conform as well as steel. So about five years ago, we ditched the red metals—copper, brass, and bronze."

Harrell says, "If someone who uses one of our saws isn't smiling by the end of the cut, we haven't done our job. We're only as good as the last saw that leaves our shop."

You can order a Bad Axe saw with a small, medium, or large tote in a variety of hardwoods. The current Bad Axe lineup of a dozen backsaws, panel saws, and frame saws ranges from a ten-inch luthier's saw (meant for making fret-wire cuts on a guitar neck) to a thirty-six-inch frame saw modeled after one depicted in André-Jacob Roubo's *L'art du menuisier*. Wait times range from twelve to sixteen weeks.

Florip Toolworks

Empire, Michigan
www.floriptoolworks.com

Like many other saw makers, Erik Florip developed an interest in woodworking, which led to tool buying, which led to toolmaking. Today, his Florip Toolworks produces a small line of traditional saws and marking gauges from an old pole barn on the eastern side of Lake Michigan.

"This started for me in about 2012," he tells me. "My wife wanted a bookshelf, and I thought I could make one. I began buying tools off Craigslist, and that's when I found out that there's a difference between nice tools and not-nice tools." Florip began buying old tools at estate sales. "I found that those old Western saws are really nice saws. Then I stumbled into the world of custom toolmakers and said, 'Holy cow! These are works of art.'"

He began saw-making by cannibalizing parts from old saws and marrying them to new steel plates. He laid out a tooth pattern in Microsoft Excel and pasted a printout to the steel to know where to file the teeth. "I was doing all the wrong things," he admits, but he kept at it.

When Florip and his family moved from California to Michigan, he taught himself how to use computer-aided design software with the six old CNC milling machines he had bought. "The bones are there, but the brain and nervous system are stripped out." He replaced the computers and software, bringing the machines fully up to date.

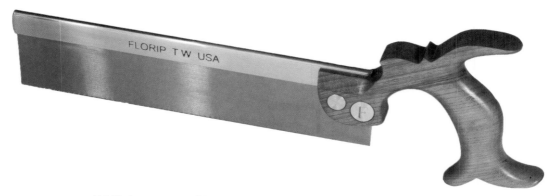

Erik Florip uses CNC machines to cut saw teeth, but does the setting and sharpening by hand.

Florip makes all the parts for his saws and marking gauges. As he says on his website, "This gives me an in-depth understanding of saw making. There is a difference between buying a set of parts for assembly and learning to make all the parts yourself."

Besides the CNC machines, his shop includes a vintage Sharp milling machine, surface grinders, a hydraulic press to fold brass sawbacks, tooth-setting machines, and a rig he built to cut saw teeth consistently. "It's a custom setup, and what it's doing and how is my little secret."

Florip doesn't aim for the high end of the market. "I thought there would be a place in the market for the hobbyist who can't justify spending a lot of money on tools," he says. "There must be a spot for someone who could make a good tool at a price that more people could afford." He seems to have had the right idea. When I spoke with him in late 2019, he said that "the business has kind of taken off. Sales tripled from last year."

The current lineup of Florip Toolworks saws consists of a tenon saw, two dovetail saws, and a small panel saw Florip calls a benchtop saw "because it never leaves my workbench." Wait times range from ten to sixteen weeks.

Florip makes all the parts for his saws, including the distinctive nut to hold the plate in place.

Profile: Marco Terenzi

Marco Terenzi makes quarter-sized tools that are practically indistinguishable from the larger originals.

A few of the people profiled in this book make small tools, but no one can match Marco Terenzi for smallness. This young Michigan native makes fully functional tools scaled to one-fourth size. In the photos on the Marco Terenzi Fine Miniatures website (www.marcoterenzi.com), he often uses a quarter for scale. Without the coin, you could easily assume that the tools are full size.

Terenzi's work reflects his lifelong fascination with miniatures and tools. "I was getting tools for Christmas when I was eight years old," he tells me. He's been collecting them ever since. In addition, he says, "I always enjoyed making detailed models, but they weren't real enough for me." So, after earning a degree in art furniture from Detroit's College for Creative Studies in 2012, he set about learning

how to make small-scale tools. He began selling his work a year later.

Terenzi makes nearly all the parts for his tools, from tiny screws and knobs to handles to hammer heads. For the saws he creates, he starts with ready-made blades, then uses "a good six hours to profile, shape, drill, and lap the blades." Little wonder that his shop equipment includes microscopes as well as a Deckel pantograph milling machine, which allows him to make accurately scaled parts from templates.

"The pantograph is the biggest game-changer in my tooling," Terenzi says. "It takes a lot of setups and a lot of templates, but it's worth it because everything comes out so well."

He uses woods like boxwood, black-wood, and mountain mahogany in his tools because they are tight-grained species that don't easily betray a tool's size.

Where other miniature makers might be content to use grinders and files to shape hammer heads from cold pieces of steel, Terenzi forges and heat-treats his. He learned blacksmithing in college and still practices it "on a super small scale." He built a miniature forge and made all his smithing tools. He even makes Damascus steel for a try square, using old files and other scrap.

For his version of the Lie-Nielsen 102 low-angle block plane, Terenzi uses a lost-wax casting process similar to what jewelry makers use. Once the bodies and caps come out of the mold, Terenzi mills and fits them, then hand files and polishes so they shine like the originals.

Terenzi typically makes one small batch of a tool, which he sells to a dedicated customer base of miniature lovers and tool collectors. After that, he's loath to make another batch of the same tool. "My mind is so over it that I don't know if I could get back into it," he says.

A few years ago, he displayed some of his tools at a meeting of the Society of American Period Furniture Makers, held at the Detroit Institute of Arts. Of course, he had the tools arrayed on a one-quarter size Roubo bench.

When I was preparing this book, Terenzi was working on a scaled-down version of a vintage Stanley square, "the kind of tool someone can relate to," he says, "the kind of tool someone probably has in his garage."

Terenzi does his own casting and forging of metal parts.

Tools for Working Wood
Brooklyn, New York
www.toolsforworkingwood.com

Joel Moskowitz is surely the only toolmaker who got his start as a museum curator. His company, Tools for Working Wood, was an outgrowth of the Museum of Woodworking Tools, which Moskowitz and a friend launched as a website in the early 1990s.

Then, on April 1, 1999, Moskowitz and his partner, Sally Bernstein, launched Tools for Working Wood, which sells its own tools as well as those from more than fifty other makers. Its first product was a workbench holdfast, which is still the company's best seller. Today, their company has two product lines—Gramercy Tools and Brooklyn Tool and Craft—as well as a manufacturing and retail outlet in an industrial neighborhood in Brooklyn, New York.

Under the Gramercy Tools banner, Tools for Working Wood sells a bow saw, either fully assembled or as a kit, as well as three traditional saws with a backed plate. The design team researched the bow-saw design thoroughly, studying every old saw they could find. As they say on the company's website, "We wanted to make sure that we understood the classic saws' engineering so as to reproduce only their best features." The Gramercy Tools saw is essentially a large coping saw whose narrow blade is meant for cutting curves.

FACING PAGE: Tools for Working Wood uses software to plan the manufacturing it will do on a CNC machine.

RIGHT: Vintage equipment like this Bridgeport milling machine work alongside modern gear.

BELOW: To assemble a dovetail saw, Naomi Baxter uses a wood paddle to whack the plate into the folded back.

TOP: The Gramercy Tools
bow saw is a design faithfully
researched and adapted from
antiques.

ABOVE: The Hardware Store
saw has handy scales on the plate
and a handle that doubles as
a square.

Brooklyn Tool and Craft sells what it calls a Hardware Store saw. It's a high-quality version of the kind of tool you can buy at a big-box store: an aggressive-cutting all-purpose panel saw, with helpful layout information and rulers etched on the plate.

The manufacturing area of Tools for Working Wood contains a small CNC machine, various grinders, turkey fryers, and toaster ovens repurposed for heat-treating steel, a Bridgeport milling machine, a vintage metal lathe, and some modern shop-made equipment for setting and filing saw teeth. However, the company outsources much of the tool-making. Various suppliers provide the parts for the bow saw, for example, as well as the brass backs and handles for the dovetail saw. Tools for Working Wood's manufacturing staff do the saw assembly, tooth setting, and sharpening at the Brooklyn location. Fitting the back on the dovetail saw means first grinding a knife edge on the plate, then whacking the tooth side of the plate with a wooden paddle to seat the steel into the opening in the brass.

On the day I visited, the crew was at the CNC machine, making prototypes of a dovetail gauge combined with a mini-square. Overhead, in a small loft, two men sat at computers writing instructions so the CNC machine could carve batches of drill bits.

"Except for the fact that we use electricity," Moskowitz says, "I don't think our procedures are different from those followed in the 1700s and 1800s. We're making new versions of old tools."

Saw Kits from Blackburn Tools

Isaac Smith, founder of Blackburn Tools (www.blackburntools.com), has a fondness for old stuff. He made his first backsaw in 2010 by cannibalizing a Disston Double Eagle from the 1840s. "The blade was all trashed. The only thing worth keeping was the spine." He copied the shape of the tote and made a new one in apple.

He launched Blackburn Tools in 2012 with a batch of backsaws, when he and his family moved from Aurora, Colorado, to Unionville, Pennsylvania, a small town west of Philadelphia. He named his company for his grandfather. In 2015, Smith switched from making completed saws to selling kits. "Selling the parts was a lot more profitable," he tells me.

Today, Smith makes his kits in a small shop a few miles from his home, using machinery that's seventy years old if it's a day. Smith says he spent five to seven years outfitting the shop with equipment he bought at tool auctions and estate sales. Trained as a structural engineer, Smith doesn't mind restoring machinery. "There's not a lot to do except clean them and replace the bearings," he told me as we looked over the parts of a drill press awaiting reassembly. "Once in a while, you'll find a broken part, so you have to go search for one or make a replacement."

Smith uses 1095 spring steel for his plates. The material arrives in one-hundred- to three-hundred-foot coils.

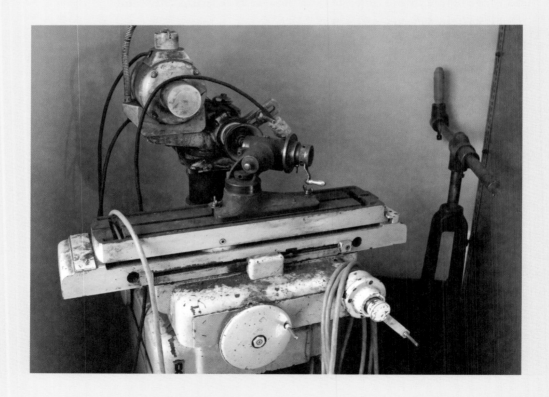

He cuts it to length on a stomp shear, a foot-powered cutter that works with a forceful downward kick on a treadle. "Sometimes I have to jump on it," he says.

To take the curl out of the steel, Smith runs it through a set of slip rollers. This hand-cranked machine applies just enough pressure to straighten the metal without compressing it.

The shop's motorized toother sits on Smith's workbench. It works with long ratchet bars to punch teeth at the proper pitch. Smith also has a kick press to tooth a saw plate. This machine has a fence that registers the plate off the just-punched tooth. Smith made a jig for the kick press that allows him to pivot the plate in a

shallow arc, producing teeth with progressive rake. A saw plate with progressive rake can start cutting easily. Progressive pitch also makes it easy to start a cut.

Smith sells kits for four types of saws: a Roubo frame saw, a Danish frame saw, a backsaw, and a panel saw modeled after one that John Kenyon made in Sheffield, England, in the eighteenth century. Smith also sells a kit for a rebate saw, a specialized tool with a short plate and an adjustable fence, used to saw a shallow kerf on all four faces of a board. Smith says that makes an easy-to-follow line to guide a frame saw. The kits include everything but wood for a tote or frame.

FACING PAGE: Isaac Smith uses eight vintage machines, like this tool and cutter grinder, to make saw kits under the Blackburn Tools banner.

ABOVE: This small Hardinge lathe turns out small brass parts. Smith says it's accurate to 0.0005 inch.

RIGHT: The aptly named kick press punches the teeth in a piece of spring steel when Smith steps hard on the foot pedal.

Hand Planes

HAND PLANES, LIKE WORKBENCHES, most likely originated in Roman times. A plane from 79 CE is the earliest known example of the tool. It looks remarkably similar to a plane that woodworkers use today. That shouldn't come as a surprise, since the plane's basic function has stayed constant over the centuries. It flattens wood or gives the edge of a board a groove or a decorative curve. The size of the plane and the cutting edge of the blade take many forms, however, reflecting the specific needs of each woodworking specialty—violin making, carpentry, barrel making, cabinetmaking, and so on.

Modern-day planes range in size from miniatures about an inch long, often meant to shape the delicate scroll on the neck of a violin, to behemoths more than two feet long for flattening the face of a large board or trueing its edge. Between those extremes are wood-bodied planes for cutting specific molding shapes; flat-bottomed planes in metal or wood (or both) for smoothing boards; narrow planes meant for cutting rabbets or cleaning up the shoulders of a tenon; router planes, with a wide base and a hook-shaped blade, for plowing dadoes or cleaning up a hinge mortise; combination planes that accept dozens of interchangeable blades; and planes meant to be used on their side, in conjunction with a workbench fixture called a shooting board, to square the end of a board or make mitered boards fit together precisely.

More than a dozen individuals and companies in the United States, Canada, the United Kingdom, New Zealand, and Australia make planes of all types. The makers featured here specialize in two main types: infill planes and wood-bodied planes.

The infill is a type of bench plane developed in the nineteenth century by two English companies, T. Norris & Son and Stewart Spiers. These planes have bodies made from thick slabs of steel or bronze that are dovetailed or pinned together and stuffed with pieces of dense hardwood to increase the plane's mass. Original Norris and Spiers planes are prized by collectors and priced accordingly. Wood-bodied bench and molding planes are the descendants of tools that joiners and cabinetmakers shaped for themselves until the late eighteenth century, when toolmaking first

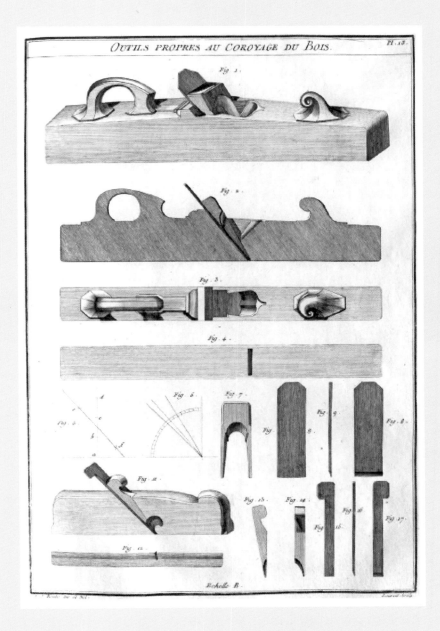

The planes that André-Jacob Roubo depicted here in 1774 would not look out of place in a modern workshop.

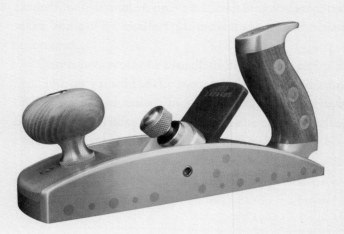

TOP: Many wood-molding planes are sprung, or designed to stop cutting when the profile is complete.

CENTER: With a full set of three dozen hollow and round planes (matched pairs with concave and convex soles), a woodworker could create or match almost any molding profile.

ABOVE: Today's plane makers feel free to reinterpret classic designs by streamlining the body or modifying the front knob, as seen in this hand plane by The Lazarus Handplane Co.

became a distinct trade. Today, most of the people making wood-bodied planes are producing sets of hollows and rounds, the all-purpose planes used to shape moldings. A hollow plane has a convex sole; its matching round has a concave sole.

Some makers, like Lie-Nielsen Toolworks (page 14), produce hundreds of planes a week. Others, notably Scotland's Karl Holtey (page 106), will spend weeks making a single plane. The materials they use include cast iron or cast bronze, stainless steel, tool steel, brass, maple, birch, quartersawn beech, and numerous tropical hardwoods.

Some of those makers believe that the world—or at least the world of plane making—fell into decline after about 1750, with the appearance of full-time toolmakers and, later, mechanized toolmaking. These people make faithful reproductions of eighteenth-century planes, updated with modern steel for the blade (properly known as an iron). Others produce improved versions of tools cranked out by the carload in the late nineteenth and early twentieth centuries. Still others use classic designs as starting points for their own creations. And a few begin with a blank sheet, completely reinterpreting what "hand plane" means.

Holtey Classic Hand Planes
Lairg, Sutherland, Scotland
www.holteyplanes.com

In the north of Scotland, in a shop near the shores of Loch Shin (Loch Ness is about seventy miles to the south), Karl Holtey started out making infill planes with Norris-style adjusters for the iron, crafted to a higher level of precision than the originals. He has now moved onto his own designs (the No. 98 series). As Holtey says on his website, "My work is regarded by many as the benchmark for these types of tools."

The first plane he made was modeled after a Norris A1. It was 15 ½ inches long and, Holtey says, "left a lot of room for improvements." Since then, his maxim has been, "Every single plane I make has to be better than its predecessors." He once wrote that his No. 983 low-angle block plane was the best he had ever made. But then he went on to make the No. 984, a low-angle jointer ("my swan song," he declares), and the No. 985 smoother.

FACING PAGE: Karl Holtey's A6 smoother follows designs that T. Norris & Son and Stewart Spiers introduced in the nineteenth century.

TOP: Holtey once said this 983 stainless-steel block plane was the best he had ever made. But he went on to outdo himself.

ABOVE: More than a dozen fasteners connect the sides and sole of the No. 985 smoothing plane. When Holtey finishes the plane, those connectors are invisible.

ABOVE: Holtey works alone in a small but well-equipped shop near a lake in northern Scotland.

RIGHT: It can take two hundred hours for Holtey to make a plane. Even with all his machinery, a great deal of handwork is involved.

BELOW: Holtey makes about a dozen planes at one go. "I don't like repetition," he says. Here, his CNC machine shapes a cap that holds the plane iron.

He has had a lifelong interest in art. "When I got out of school at age fifteen," he told me, "I could have gone to art school, but I'd have been accused of having my head in the clouds." Instead, he apprenticed briefly with a cabinetmaker, then moved on to spend "quite some years" working in joinery.

"There is quite a difference between cabinetmaking and joinery," he says. "Cabinetmaking is production work. You do the same thing day in and day out, and it becomes semiskilled work. But joinery is different every day."

He showed some interest in engineering and later became involved in prototyping for a cabinetmaker. "We'd make the jigs to do something, and we'd have to design the equipment to do the job."

Holtey began making planes in 1993 and moved into his current shop in 2005. His shop equipment includes two metalworking lathes, two milling machines (one a CNC machine), a band saw, an over/under planer, a surface grinder, a sander, and a fly press that weighs four tons and cost £18,000 (about $23,000). He also has a floor-standing drill press, a hand grinder, linishing machines (for flattening parts), a broach press, and a bobbin sander. Holtey tells me, "I say that everything I do is handmade because I have to make the tools to do the work."

Holtey can spend up to two hundred hours making a single plane, and he makes ten to twelve at a time. "I don't like repetition. I hate it," he says. "I decide on the number of planes to make and that's it."

Although he claimed he was retiring not long ago (he's in his seventies), he continues to work. "I have lots of ideas for planes. They can still be improved," he told me. For example, he's thinking about a plane that can have two different cutting angles. He has also moved away from planes with a wood infill. His last traditional plane, the T21 panel/jointer, has a body made of maple or rosewood that's dovetailed to a rosewood sole. All of his new planes in the No. 98 series are metal-bodied tools with no infill. Holtey's lineup includes a dozen infill planes and five non-infill models.

Sauer & Steiner Toolworks

Kitchener, Ontario, Canada
sauerandsteiner.blogspot.com

Trained as a graphic designer, Konrad Sauer had a ten-year-long career as an art director before he and his friend Joel Steiner began making custom infill planes. Sauer is also a hobbyist woodworker. "I started making furniture," he explains, "because I couldn't find quality furniture that would last more than a couple of years." He says he enjoyed working with hand tools, which led to a spate of tool collecting.

"One day in the mid-1990s," he says, "when I had a pretty complete set of Stanley Bedrock planes, I asked an antique-tool dealer where I should go from here. He asked if I had an infill plane. Well, I didn't know what an infill plane was. I found an old Spiers, and when I tried using it, I was immediately struck by how well it worked and by how much I enjoyed using it." At the time, vintage infill planes were expensive and sought after by dealers. So Sauer asked himself, "What's stopping me from making my own?"

Sauer and Steiner began designing a plane, working from the same basic set of drawings. Steiner soon bowed out, not wanting to give up his career. But Sauer says, "I wanted to exit the art-directing world and downtown Toronto as soon as possible."

Today, Sauer works in a two-story shop where the garage to his house once stood. The main floor houses a band saw, two jointers, a table saw, and wood storage. "Most people are struck by the fact that it looks like a woodworking shop," he says. Upstairs is the anvil, about a hundred files, and four workbenches. "I listen to what my wife calls 'very angry, raucous music.' I do my filing in time to the raucous music. It puts me in a bit of a trance and a bit of a groove."

He doesn't make planes in batches. "I tried that, but it was boring and too much like production work. I work on two planes at a time. When I get to the stage of French polishing and finishing the wood, I'll start two more. So basically I have pairs of planes leapfrogging each other." He says he makes about thirty planes a year.

For Sauer, plane making begins with the wood infill. He cuts rough blanks perfectly square, dates them, and checks every six months to see which blanks are out of square and so need more drying time. "The

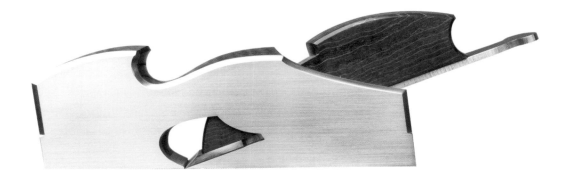

TOP: "Curves are sexy as hell," Konrad Sauer says to explain the design of his shoulder plane.

ABOVE: Sauer's coffin smoother (named for its curved sole) is only four and a half inches long.

rosewoods will expand in the summer and shrink in the winter as the humidity changes," he says. "But these woods have the ability to self-compact. They will shrink and expand one year. But the next year, the movement is less. It gets to the point where the range of movement is so small that it's imperceptible." Sauer says he has heard from customers who have had one of his planes for twenty years and seen no wood movement.

Sauer uses O1 tool steel for his plane bodies. A supplier roughs out the pieces with a water-jet cutter. Sauer does the final fitting and shaping with files and peens the sides to the sole. Ron Hock (page 139) supplies the custom plane irons.

For the first ten years or so, Sauer made planes that followed the lines of the classics. "I didn't want to be so arrogant as to think that I could

LEFT: When Sauer is nearly finished assembling a plane, he tests it to see how it will perform.

RIGHT: Sauer ages the wood for his infills for a year or more to ensure that they won't move over time and separate from the metal.

reinvent the wheel right out of the gate." But then, a customer asked him to rethink the design of a panel plane. "He'd contact me every six months to ask how things were going," Sauer says. "I was thinking about it, but nothing was happening. Then I had that lightning-strike moment. I was at my filing station, but a few feet away was a chalkboard. I walked over and drew the plane in chalk. Then I grabbed a pad and just started drawing, drawing, drawing. In the end, I had a lot of drawings and what would become the K13." He says the goal was to improve the plane's ergonomics and make something aesthetically pleasing. "I gave the body curves because curves are sexy as hell," he says.

Sauer's line includes a set of five shoulder planes and a dozen bench planes that range from 4 ½ to 18 ⅛ inches in length.

Sauer's two-story shop has four workbenches.
He listens to music as he works, saying, "It puts me
in a bit of a trance."

The Lazarus Handplane Co.
Louisville, Kentucky
www.lazarushandplane.com

A decade ago, Mateo Panzica was working as a timber framer with a side hustle. He would find old Bailey-style planes (named for Leonard Bailey, who invented an iron-adjusting mechanism) and use eBay to sell the resurrected tools. Thus was born The Lazarus Handplane Co. When Panzica decided to make new infill planes, the name stuck.

"One Fourth of July I decided to not go into the timber-framing shop," he tells me. "I drew out on paper what I wanted to do to make my own planes. I ordered a milling machine that arrived five days later." However, he says, "I'm absolutely not a machinist. I know just enough to do what I do. I consider myself an accomplished woodworker." He does have some familiarity with metal, though. "When I was a kid I went to art school in Chicago. I started figure drawing, but wound up doing bronze figurative work. I loved the craft of mold making, pouring metal."

Mateo Panzica's infill planes push form in new directions, with streamlined bodies and outsized knobs. But their essential elements, such as the adjusting mechanism, are much like their nineteenth-century forebears.

TOP LEFT: Infills and tote for a smoother ready to be finished.

TOP RIGHT: Parts for the body are roughly shaped, ready for more drilling.

BOTTOM LEFT: Principal brass and stainless-steel parts marked where they need to be drilled and tapped.

BOTTOM RIGHT: Plane body assembled with screws and metal dowels.

Today, he works in his three-car garage in Louisville, Kentucky. "It's scrappy, with really modest equipment," Panzica says. Besides that original milling machine, he has a metalworking lathe that belonged to his grandfather, a benchtop surface grinder, and the basic woodworking machinery—a table saw, a band saw, a jointer, and a planer.

He makes all the parts for the planes himself, including the screws and irons. The metal bodies are extremely thick, with sides that sweep upward from tote to toe. The knobs are outsized. He says his planes "have a lot of mass and a super low center of gravity. That's what I love about them and why they cut so well. When someone tries one of my planes, they won't realize it's taking a cut until they start seeing the fluff."

Panzica says he doesn't bother to count the hours involved in making a plane. He typically works on one plane at a time and says he produces "anywhere from zero to two" planes in a six-day workweek.

Panzica currently has twenty-eight different planes available. "It's important to me that I make planes that fit the budget of most woodworkers," he says. "I know that most professionals are working on tight margins."

Daed Toolworks

Greenfield, Indiana

www.daedtoolworks.com

Imagine a plane with a wedge shaped like a bird's wing to hold the iron. That's the main design motif of the small infill planes that Daed Toolworks makes. Raney Nelson, who founded Daed in 2010, explains that the name came from his daughter, who made him a birthday card with the word *dad* misspelled.

Working in a small town east of Indianapolis, Nelson makes three styles of planes: one roughly equivalent to a block plane, which he calls an index plane; a coffin smoother; and a miter plane. The index planes have the bird-wing wedge. The coffin smoothers use a traditional lever cap. And the miter planes have a thick wedge and a long iron that's snecked. (*Snecking* is a term borrowed from stonemasons; here, it refers to a plane iron shaped with a thick section of steel at the end.) The long iron makes a good handhold, says Nelson, and the snecking makes it easy to adjust the iron with a plane hammer.

An extra-long iron and a flamboyant wedge to hold it in place are hallmarks of the Daed Toolworks style.

Nelson's shop includes a CNC machine, which he calls "the world's best roughing machine. It can cut dovetails close, to within a couple of thousandths, then I do the handwork. The CNC gives me a lot of reference points that I wouldn't otherwise have, and it helps with uniformity. The machine lets me skip the two-thirds of plane making that I don't like." He says it takes him twenty to twenty-five hours to make a small plane.

ABOVE: A Daed miter plane has a body-machined square and is meant to be used on its side with a shooting board.

LEFT: Raney Nelson has run Daed Toolworks since 2010. He also worked with Chris Schwarz (page 45) to start Crucible Tools.

Brese Plane

Thomaston, Georgia
breseplane.blogspot.com

Like many other toolmakers, Ron Brese took up woodworking out of necessity, which led to collecting hand tools and then to toolmaking. In Brese's case, he was trying to avoid a health issue. "I became concerned with the amount of dust exposure to which I was subjecting myself," he tells me. "More planing, less sanding made a lot of sense. I really wanted better finishing planes, so the next step was to pursue infill planes in order to achieve a better surface on my furniture pieces."

Brese says he needs one to two weeks to make a plane. "Some planes just seem to want to be together," he says, "and some seem to make you earn every bit of progression that's achieved." A critical stage for every plane is squaring the bed-angle section of the rear of the sole. "It has to be flat and quite square across the width of the plane," Brese says. "Anything other than perfection at this step and the plane will never bed the iron properly."

At present, Brese says he's "sort of pursuing whims. If someone approaches me about making a plane, I propose something that would be interesting for me to make at that particular time."

Ron Brese's designs follow classic lines. The one shown here is his Winter Panel plane, with a macassar ebony tote and knob.

Bill Carter

Leicester, East Midlands, England
www.billcarterwoodworkingplanemaker.co.uk

Bill Carter, trained as a carpenter and jointer, makes infill planes that are noteworthy for two reasons. One, they are small. His tiniest is a smoother just an inch long; the largest is barely bigger than a block plane. Two, he's the only maker who shapes his dovetails into curves he calls cupid bows. He repeats the cupid-bow motif on the bridge that helps anchor the wedge for the iron.

Carter began making wood-bodied planes for himself in the 1970s. At the time, he was a cabinetmaker at the Leicester Museum and Art Gallery. That's where he saw his first Norris plane. "I said to myself, 'I have to have one of these,'" he tells me. It took him a year, but he found a Norris A5 for £10 (about $13).

He began making infill planes in 1983 and took up full-time plane making four years later. He guesses that he's made a thousand planes over the years. This includes hundreds of miniature smoothing planes he calls Little Billies. The sole is only 1 ⅜ inches long and requires sixty tools to make. Some of his smallest planes are made from the brass backs of old tenon saws.

Carter now works in a small, unheated shed he built several years ago. The only machines he owns are a grinder and a small band saw. Otherwise, he makes his planes by hand, using hacksaws, hammers, and files. He needs about a week to make a plane up to six inches long; it takes a couple of days longer to make larger planes, he says.

TOP: Bill Carter works entirely with hand tools to make this seven-inch-long miter plane.

CLOCKWISE FROM ABOVE LEFT: He clamps the bronze body in a vise and uses a crowbar to slowly bend it around a form. He hacksaws and files the dovetails for a precise fit. He shapes his unique cupid-bow dovetails by eye, using a series of small files.

BJS Planes and Woodworking
Melbourne, Victoria, Australia
www.bjsplanesandwoodworking.com

Brian Shugarue grew up in Newfoundland, where he studied forestry and natural resources and worked in various outdoors jobs. He moved to Calgary, Alberta, in 2001 to begin a four-year cabinetmaking apprenticeship. "My first-year instructor had a wood plane that would just sing," he tells me. "It was appealing." Appealing enough for Shugarue to begin making his own planes.

In 2008, Shugarue and his wife moved to Australia, where she had taken a job. He continued to work in the cabinetmaking trade, but still wanted to make planes as a hobby. One day, he passed a newsstand and saw a British woodworking magazine with Bill Carter (page 120) on the cover. "I asked myself, 'What's holding me back from making infill planes?'" He bought a drill press and got started. He says he would work long hours in the building trades, then put in time on nights and weekends making planes.

A decade later, Shugarue launched BJS Planes and Woodworking to begin plane making full time. He makes four sizes of a low-slung smoother that he designed, plus a traditional coffin smoother and a squirrel-tail infill plane based on the Stanley 101. Shugarue also makes custom designs for clients. He buys his irons from Ron Hock (page 139) and gets the parts for the plane bodies from a supplier who cuts them to rough shape with a water jet. Shugarue then cuts the dovetails in the metal by hand with a hacksaw and files. He spends seventy-five to eighty-five hours filing and fitting the parts.

"I just love experimenting with different wood and side materials," he says. "I currently enjoy working with Damascus steel and *mokume-gane*." (*Mokume-gane* is a Japanese metalworking technique that produces wood-grain-like patterns on a steel surface.) "The wood is always the most exciting part," he says. "I love showcasing beautiful Australian timbers because so many lovely dense and stable species grow here."

Shugarue makes one plane at a time on a commission basis. He currently has a one-year waiting list.

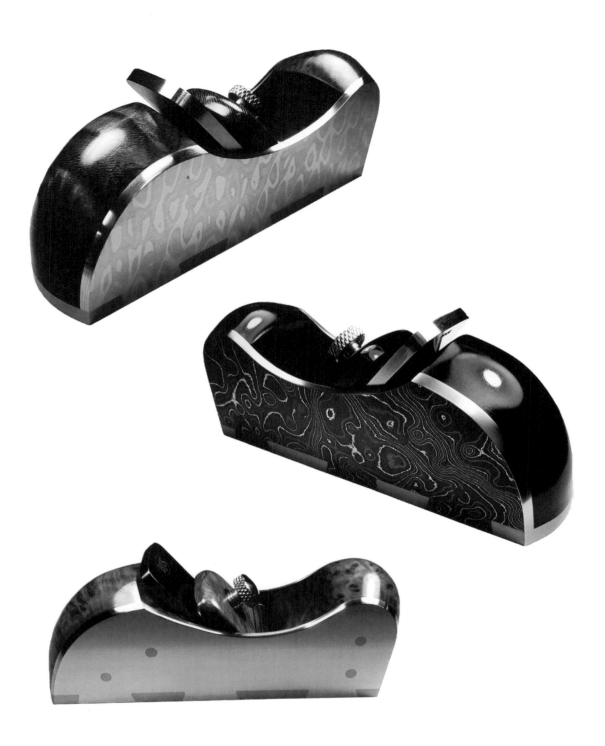

TOP: For this unique smoother, Brian Shugarue uses steel made with *mokume-gane*, a laminating technique that produces a surface resembling wood grain.

CENTER: Shugarue uses Damascus steel for some planes. A us company supplies that material.

BOTTOM: Shugarue says his favorite material for infills is ringed gidgee, an Australian hardwood.

Old Street Tool
Eureka Springs, Arkansas
www.planemaker.com

Larry Williams and his partners have been making wood-bodied planes in the small town of Eureka Springs, Arkansas, for close to thirty years. In that time, their company, Old Street Tool, has become enormously influential. When I talk about planes with other plane makers, Old Street is usually the first name that comes up. Williams is also widely acknowledged as the force behind the renewed interest in eighteenth-century planes. More than three hundred Old Street planes are used at Colonial Williamsburg, the bastion of life and work in the 1700s.

When I asked Williams why eighteenth-century planes are so good, he answers immediately. "They're like sports cars. They have better proportions. They fit your hand better. You're not struggling with the plane and can focus on your work."

And as Old Street explains on its website, "From the early 1800s development efforts appear to be aimed at reducing labor costs, and those reductions translated to a steady decline in the quality of wooden planes.... Some of the changes include standardizing wedge thickness to two or three sizes, a less comfortable shortened grip, ill-advised introduction of early machine production, and reducing efforts at chamfering and shoulder details. Each of these had cascading results that impaired the function, feel, and quality of the planes."

Williams and Don McConnell, his partner since 2005, make everything for their planes. They shape and heat-treat O1 tool steel for the irons and make the bodies from quartersawn beech. Once plentiful, beech is now expensive and sometimes hard to come by. But that hasn't fazed Old Street. "We never considered anything other than beech," Williams says. "It's ideal for plane making." It's fairly dense, giving the plane the mass it needs, and stable, so the profile of the sole won't change.

Williams and McConnell once made planes entirely by hand, but they now use some machinery, such as a band saw and two Grizzly wood mills. "We have introduced machinery, but we don't let it control the product," Williams told me.

McConnell got his start as a plane maker in Ohio, where he was working in the cabinet shop of a living history museum "with nineteenth

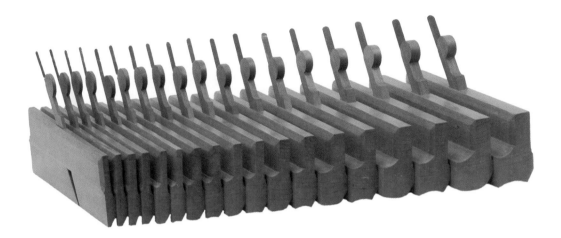

TOP: This half set of hollows and rounds from Old Street Tool is faithful to its eighteenth-century counterparts, but with irons made of modern tool steel.

ABOVE LEFT: Larry Williams, the founder of Old Street Tool, is an influential artisan who believes that plane making reached its peak in the 1700s.

ABOVE RIGHT: Don McConnell started making planes at a living history museum in Ohio. He has been part of Old Street Tool since 2005.

TOP: The Moving Fillister plane cuts a rabbet 1 ¼ inches wide. Its body, like those of all Old Street planes, is made of quartersawn beech.

CENTER: The Old Street smoother has an iron of o1 tool steel, which Williams and McConnell shape and heat-treat in house.

ABOVE: Old Street's Strike Block plane is essentially a large miter plane, meant to be used with a shooting board.

century planes, I might add," he says. "I had done period-furniture making and some high-end architectural woodworking, but I got to the point where I couldn't physically do some of the heavier woodworking. Then I met Larry and saw that we had shared interests."

Williams started a career as an architectural woodworker in the mid-1970s. He began making planes for his own use, as well as the coarse files called floats that are used to shape the throat of a wood-bodied plane. He and an earlier partner, Bill Clark, took up plane making in 1996.

Old Street has fifteen products in its line. The bench planes range from a 6 ⅝-inch coffin-shaped smoother to a 30-inch jointer. Grecian ovolo molding planes are available in six sizes. The company also offers a half set of hollows and rounds (nine matched pairs).

This plow plane is a descendant of nineteenth-century planes, such as the Stanley 45 and 55, with interchangeable irons. Old Street's version comes with seven irons for cutting rabbets or dadoes.

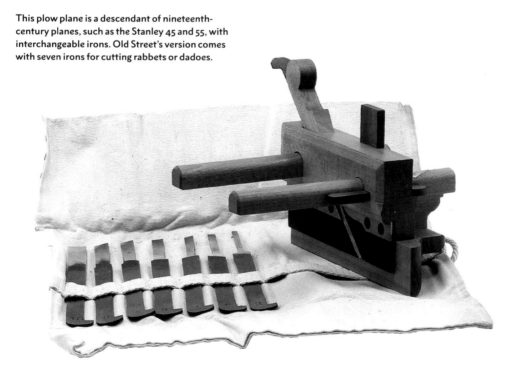

M. S. Bickford

Haddam Neck, Connecticut
msbickford.com

Matthew Sheldon Bickford wrote the book on using molding planes. *Mouldings in Practice*, from Lost Art Press, explains how to create a series of rabbets to provide guides for the hollow and round planes that actually create a molding profile.

"I got my first set of antique planes and was aware they could do anything, but I couldn't do anything with them," Bickford tells me. "I came up with a process to get the results I wanted. As I started selling planes and pursuing customers, I'd describe my process." With some encouragement from Christopher Schwarz (page 45), Bickford produced *Mouldings in Practice*. Now, he says, "The book has turned into a big thing for me. It's something to point people to."

Bickford began making planes professionally in 2010, following a ten-year career as a derivatives trader. He had taken up woodworking as a hobby and was using a variety of router bits to make moldings. He also watched a film by Larry Williams (page 124) on making a plane. He made several. "They worked better than any antique I had tuned," he tells me. After some prodding by another woodworker, Bickford made a batch of planes. "I was hoping one person would buy a plane," he says, "but five or six people said yes."

Today, Bickford and his family live in rural Connecticut. His shop occupies one room on the second floor of his house. A band saw, a jointer, and a planer take up most of the floor space. A sharpening bench sits in one corner. Bickford's workbench is nearby, positioned in front of a large window. His grinding gear is in the basement, off-limits to visitors.

On the day I visited, Bickford was completing a half set of hollows and rounds for a customer. He had finished all eighteen bodies and ground the irons to match the planes' soles. Today he would do the final sharpening of the irons.

Customer feedback has led Bickford to change the way he sharpens. People often resharpen his irons, changing the original edge in the process. When the customers complained that the plane wouldn't perform well, Bickford would have to resharpen the iron. These days, he sends his

TOP: Matthew Bickford assembles and tunes his planes at a bench overlooking the front yard of his Connecticut home.

LEFT: Bickford left a career in finance to take up plane making full time. He has made four thousand planes (and counting).

ABOVE: Two shelves of planes serve as patterns for Bickford, who says that hollows and rounds are his favorites.

LEFT: After shaping the iron and honing it razor-sharp, Bickford makes a few test cuts to see how the plane performs.

RIGHT: A paper-thin shaving from the brand new plane.

planes out with a mirror finish on the back of the irons, which makes people think twice about resharpening them.

Lie-Nielsen Toolworks (page 14) supplies the O1 tool steel blanks for M. S. Bickford irons. Bickford does his own grinding and heat-treating. In an average week, he says, he spends one day grinding and heat-treating the irons and another day sharpening them. He needs only a couple of hours to shape a plane body from quartersawn beech. On average, he makes about two planes a day, and he has made close to four thousand in his first ten years of business.

Although Bickford will fulfill a customer's request for a molding plane with a specific profile, hollows and rounds are his first love. Antique hollows and rounds as well as the ones Bickford makes today have soles based on a sixty-degree arc. "The planes make a specific arc, not a specific profile," he explains. "This means the planes can reproduce any old molding." This leads him to a discussion of infinite possibilities. Machinery has its limits. "If you have a six-inch jointer, you'll want an eight-inch. And if you have an eight-inch jointer, you'll want a twelve-inch. But if you work with hand planes, you can flatten any width of board. Similarly, hollows and rounds let you reproduce any shape of molding."

The Place for Plane Parts

Mesa, Arizona, is the home of the curiously named St. James Bay Tool Company (stjamesbaytoolco.com). It's run by Bob Howard, who has been machining parts for hand planes for close to forty years. Originally from Long Island, New York, he participated in Revolutionary War reenactments, which led to making period furniture as a hobby, which led to antique-tool collecting. Trained as a machinist, Howard made new parts for some of his vintage finds. Fellow tool collectors began asking him to make parts for them, too. Before long, Howard was in the plane-parts business.

When the aerospace industry slowed on Long Island, Howard moved his family to Arizona. He's been working there for the past twenty-five years, selling plane kits, replacement parts, and vintage tools, and doing custom work for clients. "I'm constantly getting requests for this or that," he told me.

Howard works in his three-car garage (which he shares with his wife's car). His equipment includes two Bridgeport milling machines, two lathes, and plenty of woodworking machinery—some fifty pieces of equipment in all. Everything is on mobile bases, he says, "so I can reconfigure things in a matter of minutes."

TOP: Bob Howard set up shop in his garage, which houses some fifty pieces of equipment.

ABOVE: A small selection of the vintage tools and replacement parts available from St. James Bay Tool Company.

Philly Planes
Broadstone, Dorset, England
www.phillyplanes.co.uk

Like many of the other plane makers, Phil Edwards of Philly Planes bases his bench and molding planes on antique originals. He bought all the books he could find to research plane designs. He also measured old planes and made dozens of prototypes. "It was very enlightening to make a low-angle plane and a high-angle plane and try them out," he says. "But a lot of those prototypes wound up keeping the shop warm."

A hobbyist woodworker, Edwards got his start in plane making by writing a how-to article for *Good Working* magazine about making a jack plane. He wrote eight or nine more articles, then went into plane making full time when he lost his day job. "Financially, it was not the cleverest move, but it was just the sort of kick in the pants that I needed," he tells me.

Today, Edwards's shop occupies the two-car garage at his house in Broadstone, a village just a few miles from the southern coast of England. Edwards says the shop is "a cozy little work space" that houses a table saw, a metalworking lathe, a milling machine, and a sander, among other equipment.

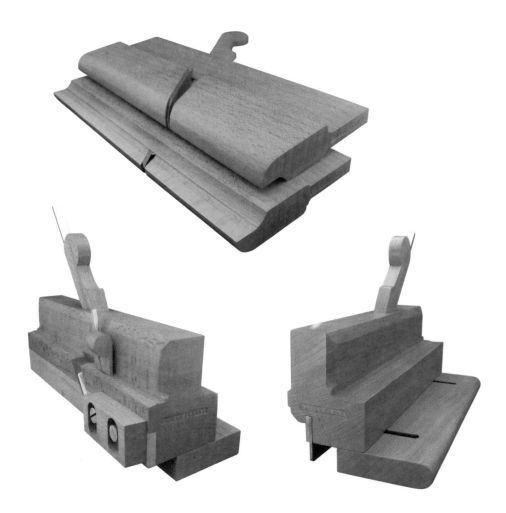

FACING PAGE: The Philly Planes panel raiser makes raised panels for doors, drawer bottoms, and the like. The iron is set at an angle to help the plane make clean cross-grained cuts.

TOP: Side-round planes cut a quarter circle, for adding detail to profiles made with hollows and rounds.

ABOVE LEFT: Philly Planes makes a unique dovetail plane, with an angled cutter that produces the male portion of a sliding dovetail joint.

ABOVE RIGHT: This small plow plane is well suited for cutting the groove that houses a drawer bottom.

Edwards makes his planes one at a time. He makes the body first, then creates an iron to fit from O1 tool steel. He needs two days to make a plane. "Every order is different, which keeps the interest level up for me," he says. "The main problem with batch work is the boredom factor."

The Philly Planes line consists of eighteen planes. There's a three-to four-month backlog.

J. Wilding
Loveland, Colorado
www.jwildingplanemaker.com

Jeremiah Wilding, owner of J. Wilding, makes a wide variety of planes based on eighteenth- and nineteenth-century patterns. "I made my first plane when I was twelve," he says. "I've always woodworked. I started as a pattern maker and spent some time in timber framing. But all that time, I was making period furniture."

Today, Wilding makes planes to order from a shop in Loveland, Colorado, about fifty miles north of Denver. Unlike most other makers of wood-bodied planes, Wilding uses quartersawn maple. His line of eighteenth-century-style planes includes a typical assortment of bench planes as well as hollows and rounds. He also makes several fillister and plow planes. These contraptions are meant for cutting a dado or rabbet; they have a stout adjustable fence, a depth stop, and a nicker—a blade that slices the wood fibers so the plane iron makes a clean cut.

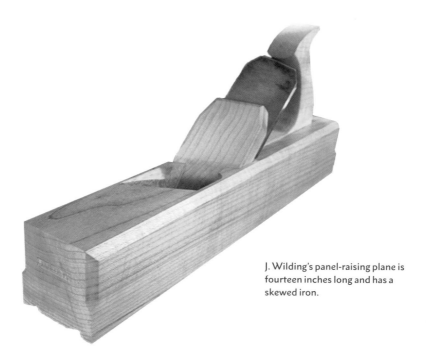

J. Wilding's panel-raising plane is fourteen inches long and has a skewed iron.

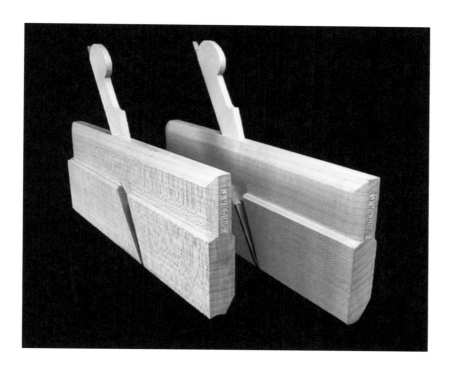

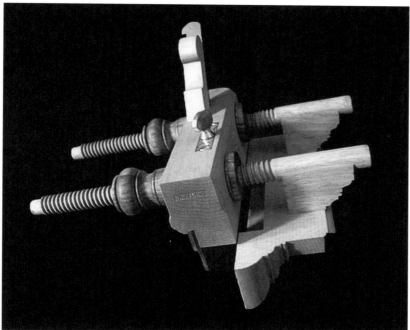

TOP: A hollow and round pair from Wilding, based on an eighteenth-century design.

ABOVE: The screw arm plow plane is an elaborate, adjustable tool for cutting grooves. The round nuts at the end of the threaded arms hold the fence in place.

Voigt Planes

Allentown, Pennsylvania
www.voigtplanes.com

Since 2015, Steve Voigt has run Voigt Planes, working in the two-car garage at his house in Allentown, Pennsylvania. The first thing I noticed when I walked into Voigt's shop was his Roubo bench. He built it from Southern yellow pine, a very durable wood that's also soft enough to be gentle on chisels.

Voigt was a music student at the University of California, San Diego. "I had a part-time job in the machine shop on campus, partly to make money and partly for access to the tools so I could make instruments. After I got my degree, I stayed full time as a machinist." Later, he took up woodworking. "I couldn't afford nice tools or nice furniture, but my experience in the machine shop gave me the confidence to know that I could make both of those things."

The centerpiece of Steve Voigt's shop is this Roubo bench, where he assembles and tests his wood-bodied planes.

TOP: Racks on the shop wall hold Voigt's floats and chisels, several of which he made.

ABOVE LEFT: Voigt sets the iron in a bench plane with a few gentle taps from a lightweight hammer.

ABOVE RIGHT: Voigt tests a smooth plane on a thick piece of maple.

To shape a plane's cap iron, Voigt clamps a piece of
steel in a fixture, then pushes until the steel touches the
wall. It's low-tech but effective.

Voigt says that Old Street Tool (page 124) was a big influence on his
work. "We both make modern tools based on eighteenth-century exam-
ples, rather than making strict historical reproductions," he says. "Old
Street makes planes with a variety of design details from the early eighteenth century. I do the same with planes from the second half of the
eighteenth century to the early nineteenth century."

His planes are double-iron designs; that is, they have a cap iron,
reflecting a major development in plane design that dates to the 1700s.
"Woodworkers in the late eighteenth century viewed the cap iron as revolutionary technology that controlled tear-out better than any other
method," Voigt says. "One of the things that led me to go into business
was that I strongly believe a double-iron plane is superior to a single-iron.
No one was making those kinds of planes, and I wanted to make them."

Voigt has O1 tool steel irons custom-made to his specifications by
Lee Valley (page 20), but he makes his own cap irons. He has a singularly
low-tech way of shaping his cap irons. He clamps a blank of steel between
two thicker pieces of metal, and then he clamps the assembly into a fixture next to one wall of his shop. Then he leans in and pushes until the fixture touches the wall. He unclamps the newly bent cap iron and takes a
step to the right, where he can finish the piece on a set of grinders. "A lot
of the methods I use seem pretty primitive, but the results are extremely
precise," Voigt says.

Like others, Voigt makes planes to order. He currently offers rabbet
and dado planes, coffin smoothers, a jack plane, and a try plane. Voigt
Planes has a four-month backlog.

Profile: Ron Hock

If you're a savvy buyer of vintage Stanley hand planes, the first thing you do after cleaning a plane and trueing its sole is throw away the old iron and buy a new one from Ron Hock (www.hocktools.com).

Hock is the first to acknowledge that he owes his blade-making career to James Krenov (page 153). Hock once told me he was "busy going broke" trying to sell his knives at craft fairs when Krenov's son-in-law asked him to make irons for the planes that Krenov's woodworking students used. At the time, in 1982, Hock says he knew almost nothing about planes, but he proved a quick study. He soon found a wide market for his thick irons made from O1 and A2 tool steel. He now subcontracts the majority of his manufacturing to a French factory, with whom he has a longstanding relationship.

For more than thirty years, Hock and a couple of helpers worked from a backyard shed filled with vintage milling and grinding equipment. In 2014, he moved his operation to larger quarters on the main street in Fort Bragg, California.

Hock sells, in addition to irons for Stanley planes and Krenov-style planes, marking knives, kitchen-knife kits, spokeshave blades, and plane kits. If you phone to place an order, chances are good that Hock himself will pick up on the first ring.

Using World War II–vintage machinery, Ron Hock has been making plane blades since 1982. He supplies the irons for many of the other makers in this book.

Red Rose Reproductions

Sterling, Illinois

redrosereproductions.com

Dan Schwank, owner of Red Rose Reproductions, makes eighteenth-century planes with twenty-first-century equipment. Trained as a machinist, he roughs out plane bodies on a milling machine with fixtures he designed. "I saw the mouth and rough the mortise with the milling machine," he says. What once involved twenty minutes of handwork now takes five. However, Schwank finishes the bodies the old-fashioned way, using his collection of twenty floats.

The blades in Red Rose planes are O1 tool steel. Schwank's former coworkers at a tool and die shop taper the steel for him. He does the grinding, heat-treating, tempering, and sharpening.

His first product was a spill plane, which makes a tightly curled shaving that was used to transfer a flame from a fireplace, say, to a candle or a lantern. "They're easy to make and quick. I can sell thirty or forty of them in the last three months of the year," he tells me.

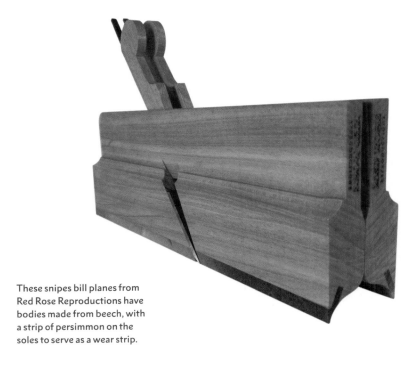

These snipes bill planes from Red Rose Reproductions have bodies made from beech, with a strip of persimmon on the soles to serve as a wear strip.

TOP: A spill plane produces a tightly a curled shaving, which can be used like a match to light a flame.

ABOVE LEFT: The Red Rose panel-raising plane is shorter than those from other companies, making it easier to control on small pieces.

ABOVE RIGHT: In addition to its complete planes, Red Rose Reproductions sells plane kits and plans.

Today, Schwank's lineup includes a pair of match planes to cut a tongue and its mating groove on the edge of a board; a plane to cut a cock bead, a decorative molding applied to the edge of a drawer front; planes to cut beads of various sizes on the edge of a board; and three sizes of rabbet planes. He also sells spill-plane kits, cap irons developed in conjunction with Steve Voigt (page 136), and the sector proportioning tool developed by Paul Peters (page 54).

Blum Tool Co.

see page 56

——

Gary Blum turned hand plane design upside-down. On a conventional bench plane, the blade is fixed to a slanted piece of metal called a frog. Screws allow the user to change the position of the blade on the frog, and the frog on the plane body. (The piece is named for its position next to the throat in the plane's sole, as in "I've got a frog in my throat." Such is plane-maker humor.)

Blum set out to design a plane with a blade that was easy to position and easy to sharpen. He came up with a bevel-down blade and a tool that's "conventional in all the normal ways," he tells me. "But the frog is held at a reverse angle, and the frog also serves as the chip breaker." Unlike other plane blades, which are up to five inches long, Blum's blade is less than an inch long.

Blum also makes the Sharpening Box, a patented fixture that reverses the normal method of sharpening. Blum's box holds a tool bevel up at a precise angle, so that you can rub an abrasive stone over the tool.

Blum makes a wide variety of wood-bodied planes, ranging from a low-angle block plane to a twenty-six-inch jointer. At the end of 2019, he introduced a line of infill planes, with bodies made of steel, stainless steel, or brass and the infill made from mesquite.

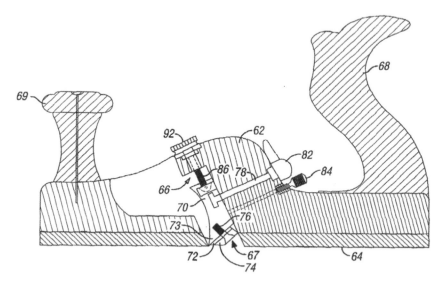

The patent drawing for Gary Blum's bench plane, which essentially turns conventional designs upside down.

Bridge City Tool Works

see page 25

John Economaki developed a hand plane to address one basic truth: one blade angle will not work well on every piece of wood. Sometimes, you need a plane with an angle of about twelve degrees; other times, an angle between forty-seven and fifty degrees will work best. It depends on how tricky the wood grain proves to be.

Until recently, to get different angles you would need to buy different planes. In 2005, Economaki introduced the VP-60, a conventional-looking plane with a mechanism that can tilt the blade through a thirty-degree arc. A scale on the sole lets you set the blade to the precise angle you want.

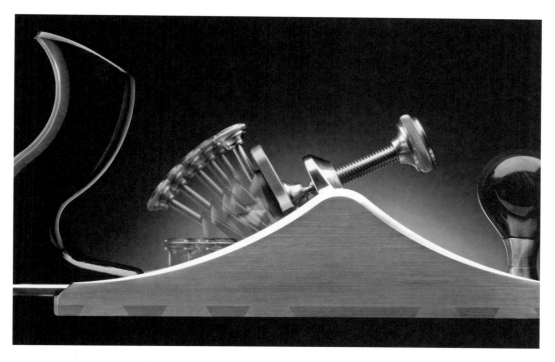

John Economaki designed the Bridge City VP-60 plane with a blade that can be set at various angles, obviating the need to have different tools on hand.

HNT Gordon & Co.
Alstonville, New South Wales, Australia
www.hntgordon.com.au

The Australian firm HNT Gordon & Co. has an extensive line of wood-bodied bench and molding planes. Two of its designs are noteworthy. Their shoulder planes are a unique infill style, with a gidgee-wood infill fitted into a U-shaped brass channel. The company also produces several bench planes that resemble Japanese planes and work on either a push or pull stroke. The inspiration for these was a similar type of plane used by a Chinese woodworker whom founder Terry Gordon had met in Malaysia.

Gordon grinds all his irons with a thirty-degree bevel, but beds the irons at different angles in different planes. Most of Gordon's plane bodies are made of gidgee, a wood twice as dense as beech. Gordon harvests his own wood "looking for the straightest trees we can get." He dries blanks in his large kiln for six to seven weeks, then drills the blanks for alignment rods and glues on brass wear strips. These blanks sit for twelve to eighteen months. "When we pull a piece off the shelf, all the stresses in the wood are gone," Gordon says.

The Gordon family (father, daughter, and two sons) work in a modest shop in southeastern Australia. Here, one of them puts the finishing touches on a molding plane.

TOP: HNT Gordon uses gidgee for this bench plane. The company harvests the wood in western Australia and kiln dries it for six to seven weeks.

CENTER: Handles on this smoother allow it to be used on the push or pull stroke.

ABOVE LEFT: The company uses brass pieces, called abutments, as wear strips on many of its planes.

ABOVE RIGHT: Molding plane bodies cut from various Australian hardwoods plus all the brass parts needed to assemble them.

Scott Meek Woodworks
Asheville, North Carolina
www.scottmeekwoodworks.com

Scott Meek never studied at the College of the Redwoods but was greatly influenced by James Krenov (page 153) nonetheless. In 2008, with the recession killing his cabinetmaking business, he found *Making and Mastering Wood Planes*, by David Finck, with a foreword by Krenov. "I grabbed a block of wood and a Ron Hock blade and made a plane," Meek tells me. He posted a photo of the plane on a woodworking forum, where a tool collector saw it and bought the first three planes Meek made. Meek took his planes to a Woodworking in America conference and to a Handworks show (see Benchcrafted, page 38). "I had such an amazing response to my planes at Handworks that I became a full-time plane maker," he says.

LEFT: Scott Meek offers buyers a choice of highly figured woods for planes like the smoother shown here.

BELOW: You can order a jack plane carved with either a right-hand or left-hand grip, in tiger maple, white oak, or mesquite.

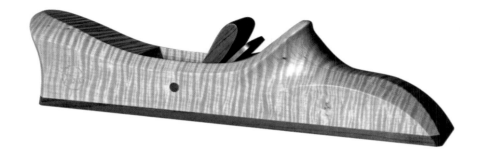

TOP: Meek also offers a kit for a twenty-two-inch jointer made from high-quality plywood.

ABOVE LEFT: Even small planes need several clamps for a proper glue-up.

ABOVE RIGHT: Two tiger maple jack planes await a coat of finish. Other blanks—including blue-dyed maple for a block plane—await glue-up.

LEFT: A book by David Finck, one of James Krenov's students, inspired Meek to take up plane making.

Benedetto

Savannah, Georgia
www.benedettoguitars.com

Chances are if you know Bob Benedetto, you know him as a leading maker of acoustic arch-top guitars. But in recent years he has launched a second career as a maker of palm planes for carving the inside and outside arches of guitar tops and backs, as well as for general woodworking.

Benedetto makes two models: one with a flat sole and one with a sole that is double radiused (heel to toe and side to side). The body of the flat sole model is 3 ½ inches long, while that of the radiused-sole model measures 3 ¼ inches. He glues up the bodies from "hard, curly Northeastern sugar maple." A ¼-inch-thick brass holding cap pivots on a ³⁄₁₆-inch brass cross pin to hold the iron in place. The radiused sole model has a ½-inch-thick brass toe and a ⅛-inch-thick brass ramp. A maple palm rest affords the user comfort and full control while using these one-handed planes, Benedetto explains. He makes all the parts for his planes except the irons, which he has custom made by Ron Hock (page 139).

ABOVE: Bob Benedetto's flat-soled palm plane is the larger of the two models he makes.

RIGHT: The curved-sole model is radiused front to back and side to side. The large palm rest on both planes makes for comfortable one-handed use.

The palm plane is the result of a decades-long love of guitars and guitar making. Benedetto made his first plane in 1969, using maple that he cut from his family's rock-maple kitchen table and a putty-knife blade that he reground. "It held an edge beautifully and I used it my entire career," he says.

Benedetto makes his planes in batches—he had fifty under construction when I spoke with him. He sells them through two online retailers of musical-instrument equipment: StewMac (www.stewmac.com) and Luthiers Mercantile International (www.lmii.com). Benedetto says he has a one-year backlog.

BELOW: Before Benedetto was a plane maker, he earned a reputation as a skilled maker of arch-top guitars.

RIGHT: Benedetto makes his planes in large batches, sometimes fifty at a clip.

Walke Moore Tools
Rochester, New York
www.walkemooretools.com

Edward Preston made planes in nineteenth-century Birmingham, England. Among his many products was a unique router plane whose cutter and knobs could be switched to any one of four positions to get into otherwise hard-to-reach places. This plane, the Preston 2500P, is prized by collectors but very hard to find.

Enter Alan Walke and Aaron Moore, who founded Walke Moore Tools in 2012. After attending some Lie-Nielsen Hand Tool Events and one of the Handworks get-togethers, they decided to begin plane making. "We were looking for a niche tool," Walke says, and they settled on an improved version of the Preston 2500P. The pair managed to find an original Preston to use for prototyping, and sold their first router plane in 2015.

ABOVE: Walke Moore Tools sought a niche in the hand plane market and settled on an improved version of a nineteenth-century router plane.

FACING PAGE: A batch of planes assembled and ready to be shipped.

To better the performance of the tool, Walke and Moore incorporated several subtle changes, most notably a custom-designed cutter with a blade that can be rotated in ninety-degree increments without removing the cutter or using any tools. "This allows our router to be used in ways the Preston never could, like for large overhanging cuts or cleaning up tenon cheeks," Moore says. When we spoke, the company was transitioning from a cast-bronze body to one machined from steel.

Walke and Moore live on opposite sides of town in Rochester, New York. Walke works in the cabinet shop of a local museum, and Moore is a mechanical engineer. A mutual friend from their church introduced them. "Everything we do is one-hundred-percent American made," says Moore. "Most of it is Rochester made. There's still a lot of manufacturing here."

Profile: James Krenov

James Krenov's career as a furniture maker, teacher, plane maker, and author spanned more than sixty years.

James Krenov (1920–2009) spent six decades as a woodworker, author, and teacher. He wrote five books, beginning with *A Cabinetmaker's Notebook* in 1976 and ending with *With Wakened Hands* in 2000. They describe an almost mystical approach to creating furniture that continues to affect the way people approach tools, materials, and the process of cabinetmaking. "I always think of wood as being alive," he wrote in *A Cabinetmaker's Notebook*. "Sometimes, when I work, this creeps into the atmosphere: the sense that maybe the wood and the tools are doing, and want to do, something which is beyond me, a part of me, but more than I am."

In 1981, Krenov founded the woodworking program at the College of the Redwoods, in Fort Bragg, California. There, for more than twenty years, he held forth from a bench in the back of the classroom, training twenty students a year. One of the first things his students did was make a wood-bodied plane like the ones he used. The woodworking program is still going strong and has been renamed The Krenov School in his honor.

I interviewed Krenov in 2007 for a *Fine Woodworking* video piece about the twenty-fifth anniversary of his College of the Redwoods program. The Krenov I met was frail and nearly blind, but still full throated. Then, he was making planes largely by feel. "What I do is shape them until they are comfortable for me," he said, "with the thought that if they're comfortable in my hand, they'll be comfortable in someone else's." He went on to give me a short but vivid explanation of the difference between a good plane and a bad one: "An imperfect plane complains! It vibrates and your teeth are chattering. It's a tiny little vibration and the wrong sound.... It's not running your fingers over a silk cloth, it's more like tearing paper."

His furniture—cabinets on stands are his signature pieces—has the same timeless appeal as Shaker or classic Scandinavian designs. That's not surprising, since Shaker furniture had a direct influence on Scandinavian designers, and Krenov trained with Carl Malmsten, regarded as one of the founders of modern Swedish design. The proportions of a Krenov piece are perfect, the joinery flawless, and the marriage of different woods always thoughtful.

At the beginning of *A Cabinetmaker's Notebook*, he writes, "My way of working is just a long series of personal discoveries. I can't give anyone secrets.... But I can give hints, the benefit of some experience in the things that have happened to me."

Fortunately, people continue to take his hints.

Hammers, Mallets, and Chisels

W ITHOUT QUESTION, humankind's oldest tool is the hammer. Those who study these matters theorize that the first hammer was nothing more than a smooth rock wielded as many as 2.5 million years ago. It wasn't long (archaeologically speaking) before someone lashed the rock to a stick. Swinging this tool was easier on the hand and arm than gripping a rock in the palm to hit something. And it wasn't long (again, archaeologically speaking) before these early toolmakers began using differently shaped rocks and sticks to create a range of hammering tools for specific uses.

Beginning in the Bronze Age, about 3000 BCE, hammers began to take shapes we would recognize today, with a metal head fixed to a shaped wood handle. The first claw hammer, the ubiquitous tool that can both drive nails and pull them free, dates to Roman times. (So does the penny-weight system that we use to this day to define nail sizes.)

The rise of carpentry, stone carving, blacksmithing, and other specialized trades also gave rise to hammers tailored to the trades' specific needs. In very general terms, the weight of a woodworking mallet or hammer and the material it's made from will tell you what the tool is meant to do.

Brent Bailey, who learned blacksmithing in Africa, makes some two dozen different hammers. His Icon sledgehammer is on the left; one of his claw hammers on the right.

Hammers weighing around eight ounces are for giving light taps to small things, such as brads or a plane iron. Some lightweight hammers have a steel head, but others have a head of copper or bronze; these are used to adjust planes, since the soft metal won't mar the plane iron.

Hammers and mallets weighing between eight ounces and a pound are all-purpose tools. A claw hammer will pound nails and remove them. A cross-peen hammer (also known as a Warrington hammer, for the English town where it originated) is designed to drive brads or small nails. The narrow cross peen lets you start a nail without hitting your fingers. Mallets, either turned from a single piece of wood or made with a wood or metal head, are most often used to strike chisels.

Hammers weighing more than a pound are the workshop's persuaders, meant to drive a workbench holdfast into position, for example, or to help close a stubborn joint.

Hammers and mallets need something to hit, of course. Besides nails and brads, the most common target for a hammer is a chisel. Those featured here marry high-quality steel with beautiful hardwood handles, all finished to a degree that factory tools seldom match.

Old Soldier Toolworks, in Canada, sells ready-made and custom tools. Shown here, from the left: a six-ounce claw hammer, a twelve-ounce hammer in Damascus steel, and a cross-peen hammer.

Old Soldier Toolworks

Ottawa, Ontario, Canada
www.oldsoldiertoolworks.com

The three Canadian Army veterans who founded Old Soldier Toolworks share a love of blacksmithing. It's a craft they pursued as a hobby while still in the service. "The first time I got to heat stuff up and hit it I was hooked," says Nick Verbree, one of the founders. The company's first tools were marking knives and workbench holdfasts, but the vets soon expanded their line. They added hammers, then chisels made from either plain or Damascus steel.

The three (plus their intern) work in a fourteen-by-fourteen-foot shop in Ottawa. It houses a very large power hammer, an assortment of grinders, a forge, two anvils, and a large collection of hand tools. "It gets a little crowded," Verbree says.

It takes about a day to forge a claw hammer. Forging the eye (the hole in the head for the handle) is a difficult, time-consuming task, says Verbree, because it has to be done before the head is fully formed. When I spoke with him, Verbree said he had just finished a 3 ¾-ounce hammer. "Woodworkers like the little ones," he says.

Old Soldier Toolworks essentially makes hammers to order. "There are just too many ways to customize these," says the company's web site.

Making a piece of Damascus steel for a chisel or marking knife takes about twelve hours with a power hammer. Before acquiring this tool, they needed three days of hammering by hand to get what Verbree calls "a proper billet" of steel. They typically begin with a stack that consists of twenty-five layers of high-carbon steel, which they forge weld, hammer, and draw out. They repeat those operations until they have a piece of steel consisting of one hundred to two hundred layers. Then, Verbree says, "we have to get it dead flat and dead parallel."

Today, most of the company's work consists of custom orders. "We have some stock items because we need to," says Verbree, "but we don't keep a lot on hand."

LEFT: Old Soldier also makes chisels in Damascus steel. Folding and hammering the metal takes about twelve hours.

BELOW LEFT: A cross-peen hammer comes in three sizes—five, eight, and twelve ounces—with a curly maple or shedua handle.

BELOW RIGHT: The company's three Canadian Army veterans share a love of heating stuff up and hitting it—a craft they followed as a hobby while in the service.

Blue Spruce Toolworks

see page 68

Blue Spruce sells two styles of mallets: one shaped like a carver's mallet, one with a wood hammerhead. Both styles have a head of figured maple that's infused with resin. The round mallet comes in thirteen- and sixteen-ounce weights; the hammerhead mallet in sixteen- and twenty-four-ounce weights.

The company also has a large line of mix-and-match chisels that are made to order. Short-bladed butt chisels, dovetail chisels, paring chisels, and bench chisels have blades ranging from ⅛ inch wide to 1 ½ inch wide. You can mate any blade with one of five handle shapes turned from claro walnut, figured maple, African blackwood, cocobolo, or beech. The maple has been infused with an acrylic resin to harden it.

LEFT: The heads on carver's mallets from Blue Spruce Toolworks are infused with resin to help the maple withstand repeated blows.

RIGHT: A full set of dovetail chisels comes in sizes from ⅛ inch to 1 ½ inches. The beveled sides are concave, so the chisel will work into tight corners.

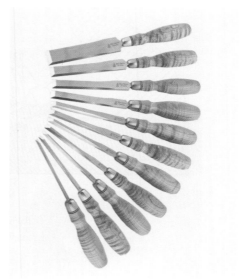

Mallets from Honduras

I helped launch a unique program to teach woodturning to artisans in a remote Honduran village. The aim was to have the Hondurans learn to make carving mallets from a variety of lesser-known woods, which Canada's Lee Valley (page 20) would retail.

The key to the collaboration was a lathe designed by a young Canadian shop teacher named Scotty Lewis. His lathe used human power—someone pedaling bicycle pedals to drive a flywheel. With the support of the American Association of Woodturners (AAW), Lewis shipped his lathe to the Dominican Republic in 2014, where he used it to teach students how to turn bowls, tops, and baseball bats.

Two years later, I helped connect AAW with another nonprofit called GreenWood. Founded in 1993, GreenWood trains artisans in Central and South America to make high-quality wood products, adding value to forest resources and creating incentives to protect biodiversity. Its artisans in Honduras have developed a diversified catalog of more than twenty-five furniture products that are sold to local markets.

Together, AAW and GreenWood brought Scotty Lewis, two of his lathes, and a Spanish-speaking member of AAW to several remote Honduran villages for two weeks of instruction. Young artisans in Lewis's workshops learned the basics of woodturning, while they vied for time "in the saddle" and competed to see who could pedal the fastest.

Over the next two years, the Hondurans honed their turning skills and tackled three key questions: What woods to use? Where to harvest them? How to dry the timbers in a tropical climate?

It took more than two years to find the right answers. By mid-2019, mallet production was well underway. One artisan, Juan Vigil, not only became a skilled production woodturner, but also turned out to be a fine teacher. He eventually had to replace the bicycle pedals on one of the lathes with a gasoline engine, a necessity to be able to produce a dozen mallets a day.

The first batch of six hundred mallets sold out in three weeks. The Hondurans continue to supply Lee Valley with mallets in three sizes and five wood species.

Thanks to support from two American nonprofit organizations, workers in a remote Honduran village have learned to turn hardwood mallets for Canada's Lee Valley.

Crucible Tool

Covington, Kentucky
www.lostartpress.com

Christopher Schwarz (page 45) is an extremely influential woodworking teacher, writer, builder, and toolmaker. In 2016, he established Crucible Tool with John Hoffman, his co-founder at Lost Art Press, and the plane maker Raney Nelson of Daed Toolworks (page 116).

Among other things, Crucible makes a unique tool called a lump hammer, the British term for a small sledgehammer. As described on the company website, "Unlike a traditional wooden mallet, the lump hammer is compact, requires less effort to use and packs considerable punch—a great asset when you need it. Plus, unlike a wooden mallet, you'll never need to replace it."

The lump hammer's alloy steel head weighs about 2 ¼ pounds and is wedge-fitted to an octagonal hickory handle. The tool is about twice as heavy as a carpenter's claw hammer, so it's light enough to strike a chisel without mushrooming the handle yet heavy enough to deliver a serious thwack when needed. "Grip the handle at its end and it can deliver a wallop that can persuade joints that have become too tight because of the glue," the Crucible Tool website explains.

Crucible Tool tries to fill small niches in the hand-tool market with products like this Lump Hammer, which delivers blows with more persuasion than a wood mallet.

Shenandoah Tool Works

Delaplane and Winchester, Virginia
www.shenandoahtoolworks.com

Norm Reid and Jeff Fleisher, who founded Shenandoah Tool Works, decided to make mallets after taking a class with the noted wood-carver Mary May. They designed a mallet with a bell-shaped steel head and initially marketed it to wood-carvers. But because the mallet can be used for other tasks, like chopping mortises, Reid and Fleisher have broadened the appeal to woodworkers as well.

Today, Shenandoah Tool Works markets mallets in brass or steel with a 1 ½-pound head and a hand-turned handle made from one of eight highly figured hardwoods. The handle has a unique hourglass shape, which allows the user to grip the mallet at the end for greater torque or close to the head for gentler taps. A foundry in Vermont supplies the heads; Reid and Fleisher make all the handles.

LEFT: Shenandoah Tool Works mallets have a head of brass or steel and a distinctive hourglass-shaped handle.

RIGHT: Holding the handle near the head, as shown here, gives you fine control for light taps. Holding the mallet at the end lets you strike with greater force.

Sterling Tool Works

Mobile, Alabama

www.sterlingtoolworks.com

Sterling Tool Works makes a unique plane hammer. It has one brass face, for adjusting the blade, and two replaceable "spuds" for adjusting the wedge on a wood-bodied plane. The spuds, made from black walnut and black nylon, screw into the brass head. A hidden Allen screw holds the handle in place.

Sterling's founder, Chris Kuehn, tells me that he decided to make the hammer after watching a skilled plane maker at a woodworking show. "I was watching him make these beautiful, beautiful planes, but he was using this butt-ugly plane hammer. I said, 'Your hammer needs to be as functional and as beautiful as your planes.'"

Kuehn gets the production parts for his hammer from trusted suppliers, doing the assembly and finishing in the shop he installed in his home's three-car garage. He also uses the space to machine prototypes of new tools.

This unique plane-setting hammer from Sterling Tool Works is widely used. The wood end, which is replaceable, strikes a plane wedge without damaging it.

HNT Gordon & Co.

see page 144

HNT Gordon & Co. makes a line of nine plane-adjusting mallets with a head weighing 150 grams, or about 5 ¼ ounces. Woods for the head include ironwood, ebony, supple jack, and ringed gidgee. A brass retaining nut holds the head and handle together.

Australia's HNT Gordon & Co. makes a line of five-ounce mallets. Woods for the head include supple jack, bull oak, pink ivory, ebony, ironwood, and ringed gidgee.

Blum Tool Co.

see page 56

Gary Blum makes a traditional all-wood mallet with a large head of hard maple and a handle of cherry or hickory. As Blum says on his website, "I patterned this mallet after an antique one I have used my whole career. The handle has flats so you can always tell the head position, and is very comfortable to hold when 'choking up' for delicate striking."

Gary Blum modeled this mallet after one he has used since he began woodworking. The head is hard maple, wedged onto a handle of hickory or cherry.

When Plain Metal Simply Won't Do

If you want something above and beyond a hammer made of steel, brass, or copper, consider one made by Seth Gould (page 77). He makes a chasing hammer (for striking small tools) and a planishing hammer (for flattening sheet metal).

The striking faces of tool steel are forge welded to a body of pure iron or wrought iron. Then Gould uses a Japanese technique called *nunome zogan* to apply 24K gold decoration. One of these babies will set you back thousands.

Seth Gould uses a Japanese technique to adorn his lightweight chasing hammer with 24K gold. Did I mention that he's trained in jewelry making?

Brent Bailey Forge

see page 200

———

Bailey makes more than two dozen styles of hammers for blacksmiths, farriers, and carpenters. Bailey's claw hammer weighs 2 ½ pounds; his framing hammer, 2 ¾ pounds.

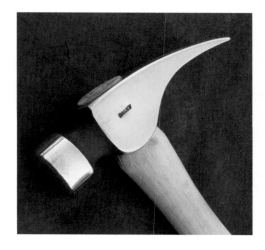

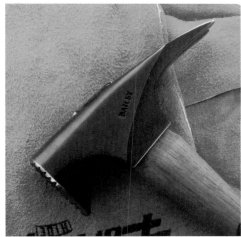

CLOCKWISE FROM TOP LEFT: Brent Bailey calls this polished claw hammer a finishing hammer; it's available in weights up to 2.2 pounds. One of his cross-peen hammers, with a head weighing up to six pounds. The patented head on his Hombre framing hammer has a teardrop-shaped face to concentrate blows. For his Rut framing hammer, he added an extra curve on the claws.

Barr Specialty Tools
McCall, Idaho
www.barrtools.com

Barr Quarton, founder of Barr Specialty Tools, got his start in the mid-1970s as a cabinetmaker in Wisconsin. One day, he picked up a book about knife making, which changed not only his career but his home. "I realized I couldn't sell these knives to the pig farmers in Wisconsin," he tells me, "so I moved to Ketchum, Idaho. I sold four or five the first day."

A few years later, he finally gave in to a friend's persistent requests to make a slick, a type of large chisel that timber framers use. That prompted his shift away from knives and into woodworking tools. An apprenticeship with a Japanese sword maker refined his forging skills.

Today, working from a shop in McCall, Idaho, Quarton turns out both slicks and cabinetmaker's chisels, as well as drawknives and other edge tools. "I still do traditional sword work, too," he says. When I spoke with him, he was finishing a short sword for a friend.

Like some other toolmakers, Quarton uses A2 tool steel for his cabinetmakers' chisels. But he hand forges the steel to compress the carbon; he says that helps the tool take a keen edge. Once he has shaped a billet, he puts the steel through three heat treatments to temper it properly, then uses a water-jet cutter to cut blanks.

Quarton makes the sockets for the chisels from steel tubing. He cuts a piece to length, then uses a plasma cutter to remove a V-shaped section. This allows him to put the steel in a die and hammer it into the socket shape. He then welds the seam closed and welds the socket to the chisel blade.

Quarton says he makes sixty to a hundred chisels a week, which barely keeps him ahead of demand. "Now we're fairly well caught up," he says, "but we're always trying to keep ahead. We'll get drawers full of one inch and inch-and-a-half chisels, but four days later they're all gone."

TOP: Barr Specialty Tools makes a set of four cabinetmaker's chisels, with ash handles and a leather tool holder.

ABOVE LEFT: Barr Quarton uses a large power hammer to forge the hot steel for his tools.

ABOVE RIGHT: Quarton makes chisel ferrules from tubing that he cuts apart, shapes, and welds to the blade.

LEFT: Quarton moved from Wisconsin to Idaho, where he began making knives, then chisels and other tools—including swords, something he learned from a Japanese craftsman.

Brese Plane

see page 118

———

Founder Ron Brese, although perhaps best known as a plane maker, says "chisels are my present fascination." He says he likes to make all the handles in a set from the same piece of wood, which can limit the size of the set. For example, he chose desert ironwood for one set, "but could only coax four handles from this piece of wood." He also says he favors "New Old Stock Sheffield England oil hardening tool steel" for the blades. Translation: he likes high-carbon steel because it holds a keen edge and is easy to sharpen. He makes dovetail chisels with relatively short, thin blades, which he says are better for paring precisely to a baseline and for reaching into corners. He grinds the sides of the blade with a sharp angle.

Ron Brese says he likes to turn the handles for his chisel sets from a single piece of wood, to match their color and figure. For the blades, he uses high-carbon steel.

The Screwdriver Makers

Gary Benson and Dave Lindeman, the two Denver-area orthodontists who founded Elkhead Tools (www.elkheadtools.com), named the company for the game they like to hunt. Both are also hobbyist woodworkers who decided to make screwdrivers because they saw that other toolmakers weren't producing them.

At first, Benson made the handles, turning hundreds on a lathe duplicator. Now, they've farmed out the work to a local company with a CNC machine. "Outsourcing the turning was a no-brainer," Benson says. "It allows us to increase quality control." The two assemble the screwdrivers and do the finishing.

Initially, Benson and Lindeman made the handles from cocobolo that they imported from Mexico. They had to switch to mesquite in 2017, when an international organization called CITES (Convention on International Trade in Endangered Species) issued a ruling that made it virtually impossible to import cocobolo. "We had to find something that was hard, durable, and available," says Benson. Now, they get their wood from a sawmill near Dallas.

Two Denver-area orthodontists who share a love of game hunting founded Elkhead Tools to make screwdrivers. Import restrictions led them to switch from cocobolo to mesquite for the handles.

Spokeshaves, Drawknives, Scorps, and Travishers

WINDSOR-CHAIR MAKING requires the use of the specialized edge tools covered in this chapter. Legend has it that the Windsor chair dates to the early 1700s, during the reign of King George I. Caught in a rainstorm during a fox hunt, the king sought shelter in a peasant's house. He was captivated by the subject's simple furniture and ordered similar pieces made for Windsor Castle. Whatever the king liked, the court liked, too, and the chair's reputation was made.

The king's Windsors resembled an easy chair missing its upholstery. Heavy cabriole legs were typical, as was a thick back rail and back splat. A cadre of master chair makers in colonial Philadelphia unquestionably gave the Windsor the form it has to this day—a lively arrangement of delicate parts that form a harmonious whole. Gracefully turned legs support a sculpted seat that's often angled for comfort. A dozen or so thin spindles support the back and arms (which, in a continuous-arm chair, are one and the same).

To my way of thinking, a Windsor chair is the consummate challenge if you're a furniture maker. Among other things, you have to know how to turn legs with shapely curves and sharp details. You have to know how to carve a comfortable seat from a large slab of wood, and how to shape spindles with a tool about the size of a machete. That's where the tools in this chapter come in.

Besides Windsor-chair makers, people who work with green wood use these tools. So do those who make period furniture (think cabriole legs or the bulbous shape of a bombé chest), Danish modern pieces, or rocking chairs modeled after the California furniture designer Sam Maloof's original.

A spokeshave is essentially a small two-handled hand plane. You use it to refine the shape of a curve and smooth the rough surface left by a saw. Some spokeshaves have a flat sole, so they work on the edge of a board or on a convex curve. Others have a curved sole, for refining a concave curve.

The drawknife is a broad blade with a handle at each end. It's meant to be used in conjunction with a shave horse—a seat with a stout,

ABOVE: Shaping the seat of a Windsor chair begins with a scorp and travisher to hog out waste in a hurry. A spokeshave refines the curves and smooths the wood.

LEFT: A drawknife, used with a shave horse, shapes spindles and can also be used to rough out stock for legs and stretchers.

foot-actuated clamp to hold the wood. You take the drawknife in both hands and pull it through the wood toward you. (Yes, a good drawknife should be razor-sharp. And, yes, you pull it straight at your heart. But, no, I've never met a chair maker who believes this is dangerous. Most say it's an extremely enjoyable part of woodworking.)

Chair makers use a drawknife to shape thin spindles or to roughly shape a piece of wood that will become a leg or a rung once turned on a lathe. Used bevel up, a drawknife will take long, thin shavings and follow the wood grain to produce a piece with continuous grain from end to end. Used bevel down, the drawknife will make fine shavings or allow you to take scooping cuts.

A scorp, also called an inshave, resembles a drawknife bent into a semicircle. It's designed to rough out the recesses in a chair seat. The word *scorp* derives from *scalper*, a Latin word for "knife."

The travisher is a spokeshave on steroids. Its big, curved sole is designed to smooth the curves on a chair seat. According to the *Oxford English Dictionary*, the word *travisher* is a variation of the word *traverse*, which may mean that the tool got its name because it can traverse, or cut across, the wood grain.

Several makers produce spokeshaves and drawknives. I was able to locate only a handful of people who make travishers and scorps.

Caleb James Maker

Greenville, South Carolina
www.calebjamesmaker.com

Caleb James moved from the Houston area to Greenville, South Carolina, in 2013. James makes Danish modern chairs and wanted to be near the rich variety of hardwoods available in the Carolinas and Appalachia. There, he got to know other chair makers, including Peter Galbert (page 185), one of the leading Windsor-chair makers in the United States.

In 2015, Galbert came to James's shop to teach a class in (what else?) Windsor-chair making. "I asked Peter what his favorite tool was," James says. "He showed me an old spokeshave, and I said to myself, 'I can make that.'" He actually made a hundred and sold them quickly.

James went on to create two more designs: a larger shave that Galbert dubbed the Monstershave, and one that James calls the Roundshave. "I've always had an issue with a spokeshave making a small radius," James explains. "On a Windsor chair, there's a part of the seat with a tight radius curve. Nothing gets in there properly. So I kept tweaking the design, and one day I got it." This spokeshave works on curves with as little as 1 ½-inch radius. "The feel is a natural carving action, much like using a carving gouge," James explains on his website.

James's work area holds six benches, "so I can have more places to put stuff." The space also includes a kiln that can dry up to a thousand board feet of lumber. "I've got enough persimmon to last me for ten years," he says.

He makes his shaves in batches of a hundred and fifty. A small shop in Canada supplies the blades, which are water-jet cut from 01 tool steel; James does everything else. Roughing a batch of wood bodies takes three to four weeks. Sanding and finishing takes two to three months. Rather than add a brass wear strip to the throat, James uses a piece of hardwood end grain.

The spokeshaves continue to sell briskly. "I'll put up thirty and sell half in the first week," James says. "By the time I make more, the others have sold."

LEFT: Caleb James developed what he dubbed the Roundshave, a spokeshave with a curved sole, for cutting in tight concave areas.

ABOVE: James began making spokeshaves after he moved to South Carolina, where he makes Danish modern chairs from a variety of Appalachian hardwoods.

ABOVE RIGHT: A tool from the master Windsor maker Peter Galbert inspired James to make what he terms the Monstershave, a spokeshave more than a foot long.

RIGHT: James makes his standard spokeshave in beech, apple, pear, or boxwood. He inserts a piece of end grain hardwood next to the blade as a wear strip.

Dave's Shaves

North Conway, New Hampshire
www.ncworkshops.com

Dave Wachnicki is a fifth-generation woodworker who grew up around millwork shops, cabinetmakers, and boat builders. He practiced as a dentist in Connecticut for ten years before moving to North Conway, New Hampshire. In 1995, his wife gave him a gift certificate for a Windsor-chair making class taught by Mike Dunbar at the Windsor Institute, about two hours south of North Conway. Wachnicki took several of Dunbar's classes and found the work a natural fit. There, he helped other students with techniques and process. Dunbar took notice and asked Wachnicki to join his crew.

For the next few years, Wachnicki was what he termed Dunbar's "graduate assistant," teaching full time. Students were required to bring a low-angle spokeshave, but many of those tools needed tune-ups or repair. Wachnicki often let the students use his homemade spokeshave while he

RIGHT: A class in Windsor-chair making led Dave Wachnicki to transition from dentistry to toolmaking.

BELOW RIGHT: With the blade recess finished, Wachnicki moves on to shaping the handles with files and rasps.

BELOW LEFT: After roughly shaping a spokeshave with a router, Wachnicki cuts the recess for the blade with chisels.

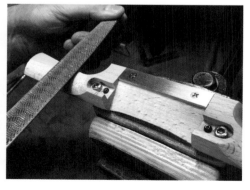

fixed theirs. More often than not, one of the students bought Wachnicki's spokeshave. Before long, that led him to begin making spokeshaves full time under the name Dave's Shaves. He stopped teaching but would periodically drop in on classes at the Windsor Institute, bringing a handful of his spokeshaves to sell. "I wanted to be sure to get there for seat day," he tells me. "That was a good day for using a spokeshave."

Working from his home in a space the size of a one-car garage, Wachnicki produces three wood-bodied spokeshaves: a standard flat-soled model with a 2 ¾-inch-long blade, a compass shave that's similar to the standard model but with a curved sole, and a smaller compass shave with a 1 ½-inch blade.

He primarily uses European beech, but also makes bodies from hard maple and cherry. Shaping begins at a router table, where Wachnicki uses one router bit and different jigs to rough out the shape of a shave. His blades, made of O1 tool steel, come from Ron Hock (page 139). Wachnicki does the final shaping with rasps and a lot of hand sanding. He finishes his spokeshaves with blond shellac, rubbed out to a satin finish.

In the past fifteen years, Wachnicki's customer base has shifted. "I still get some calls from chair makers," he says, "but decoy makers from the upper Midwest and the Chesapeake Bay area are my biggest audience these days."

LEFT: With the spokeshave body complete, Wachnicki positions the blade and wear strip.

RIGHT: On Wachnicki's spokeshaves, a small Allen wrench is used to adjust the throat for a lighter or heavier cut.

Moberg Tools
Waco, Texas
www.mobergtools.com

John Moberg of Moberg Tools says he sells most of his cast-bronze spokeshaves to a select audience—the students in his religious community's woodworking classes. "There are no unhappy customers when they can use the tool before they purchase one," he says.

The community, Homestead Heritage, has a 550-acre farm in Waco, Texas. According to its website, it is "an agrarian- and craft-based intentional Christian community" that "stresses simplicity, sustainability, self-sufficiency, cooperation, service and quality craftsmanship." Besides woodworking, it teaches blacksmithing, weaving, spinning, and pottery.

Moberg and his family live and work on a ten-acre spread a few miles from the community. When I ask him how he began casting bronze, he says with a laugh, "I was tricked into it." Then he explains, "I've been a machinist for as long as I can remember. But one of our elders, who didn't know the difference between casting and machining, thought I should teach casting. It has turned out to be a wonderful experience."

He says his spokeshaves are his favorite tools (he also makes a cast-bronze router plane). They're inspired by cast-iron spokeshaves that Stanley and Record made for decades. "I didn't invent the shape," he tells me, "I just took an existing shape and did what I thought it needed to make it better."

Some of the changes he made were practical, to accommodate the strictures of sand casting. "With a spokeshave, you have this long, skinny shape and the molten bronze has to get into all the twists and turns. So one thing I did was to slightly increase the cross-section of the handles."

In sand casting, a master pattern is pressed halfway into a frame full of fine sand. It's carefully removed, to avoid disturbing the sand, and pressed into a matching frame. The two frames are joined and the molten metal is poured into an opening in the sand, filling the void left by the master pattern. Once the metal cools, the two frames are separated and the casting removed. The sand can be reused "practically forever," Moberg says.

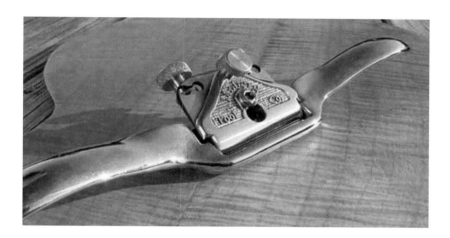

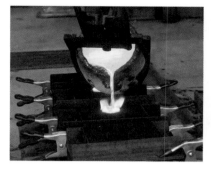

TOP: John Moberg casts a copper alloy to make spokeshaves based on vintage designs from Stanley and Record.

ABOVE LEFT: Moberg's shop contains a small blast furnace for melting metal to cast about a dozen spokeshave bodies at a time.

ABOVE RIGHT: Moberg also makes a small router plane with a cast-metal body.

The sand mixture has to be suitably moist to be an effective casting medium. Moberg uses a combination of sand, clay, and oil. Using water alone, he says, "is too challenging here in Texas because your moisture content can be just right in the morning but too dry by afternoon."

Moberg casts a dozen spokeshaves at a time, melting ingots of 873 Everdur (an alloy that's mainly copper, with small amounts of silicon and manganese) in a small blast furnace until the metal reaches 2,100 degrees. He makes his blades from O1 tool steel. Deburring, tapping screw holes, honing, milling, polishing, and buffing takes him about forty-five minutes for each spokeshave.

Moberg makes three spokeshaves: one with an adjustable blade and two low-angle models.

HNT Gordon & Co.

see page 144

——

HNT Gordon & Co. makes three spokeshaves: a large and small model with a curved sole, and a flat-soled model. All have hardwood handles connected to a brass throat section. You can order them with a tool-steel blade or a blade made from high-speed steel.

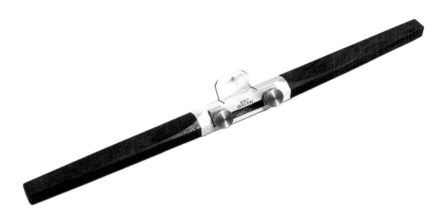

This small spokeshave from HNT Gordon & Co. can be used with the blade bevel down for cutting tight curves, or bevel up as a scraper.

Cariboo Blades

see page 198

———

Owners Scott Richardson and Aki Yamamoto produce drawknives to order, using spring steel that's either ¼ or ½ inch thick, forging the blade and tangs from a single piece. They repurpose old sawmill blades, truck springs, and the like in their work. Automobile wrecks make a good source of supply, they say. As they explain on their website, they're willing to tailor a drawknife to a buyer's desires. They offer handles in apple, walnut, yew, cherry, butternut, red mahogany, and antler. You can request handles at a specific angle. "Tell us what you need and we will build it," they say.

The couple who operate Cariboo Blades use steel reclaimed from auto springs and other sources to craft seriously heavy-duty drawknives to a customer's specifications.

Barr Specialty Tools

see page 166

Barr Specialty makes six drawknives. Curtis Buchanan—a master of the Windsor chair—designed Barr's Chair Builder model. Barr also has a smaller drawknife with what it calls "a radical bottom bevel," meant to get into tight corners on chair seats. And it makes three large drawknives that are better suited to shaping logs than chair parts. These have wide blades and are meant to be used bevel down.

Barr Quarton, the man behind Barr Specialty Tools, says he forges all the drawknives himself from 5160 steel. He used to turn all the handles, but now buys them from outside suppliers.

The scorp the company makes was designed by Mike Dunbar, another master of the Windsor chair.

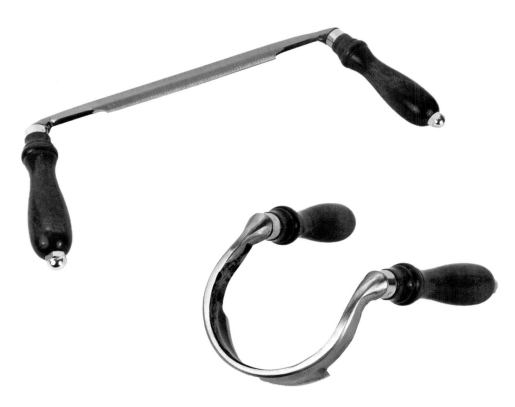

Barr Quarton's Slim Seat
drawknife, shown at the top,
is meant for shaping tight curves.
The scorp, above, was designed
by the noted Windsor maker
Curtis Buchanan.

Old Soldier Toolworks

see page 156

Old Soldier Toolworks uses 5160 steel for its drawknife, but shapes blade and handles from a single piece. As the company's website explains, "The back and edge are polished bright, but the rest of the drawknife is left rough, giving a pleasing aesthetic." The drawknives are made to order.

Old Soldier Toolworks makes drawknives to order from a single piece of steel. The company purposely leaves the handles rough to contrast with the highly polished blade.

Claire Minihan Woodworks

Portsmouth, New Hampshire
www.cminihanwoodworks.blogspot.com

Claire Minihan studied furniture and cabinetmaking at the prestigious North Bennet Street School in Boston. After she graduated, in 2010, she worked for a few years in a cabinet shop. "I got frustrated there. It was all new things and I was always learning something new," she tells me. "I knew I wanted to focus on making one thing and making it well."

In 2013, she began an apprenticeship with Peter Galbert (page 185), whom she had met at North Bennet Street. Galbert could be considered the Johnny Appleseed of travishers. He designed one with handles that curve up and out from a thick body. Over the years, he persuaded Minihan and Elia Bizzarri (see next listing) to make them. "Claire's doing a nicer job than I was," Galbert tells me. "Her travisher is like a scalpel. Now, when I need travishers, I buy them from her."

Minihan says she can make about five travishers a week and estimates that she's made eight hundred in all. She uses a variety of hardwoods, including walnut and curly maple as well as gidgee and ebony from Australia. She does her own bending and tempering of the O1 tool steel that she uses for the blade. "I know one recipe for tempering the steel and I follow it to a T," she says. She owns a small gas forge for heat-treating and uses her kitchen oven for two rounds of tempering. "I use a small loaf pan and pack the blades in tight so no oxygen gets in. It's like a Dutch oven. I heat them at four hundred degrees for an hour, then let them cool and put them in again."

Her favorite part of the process? Sharpening the blade. "It's like meditation for me. I let my muscle memory take over."

TOP: Claire Minihan learned to make travishers when she apprenticed with Peter Galbert— who says she's now the better maker.

ABOVE LEFT: Minihan makes her travishers from walnut, gidgee, curly maple, and other hardwoods. She bends, heat-treats, and sharpens the blades herself.

ABOVE RIGHT: Minihan studied woodworking at the prestigious North Bennet Street School in Boston. These days, she works from a shop in Portsmouth, New Hampshire.

Elia Bizzarri Hand Tool Woodworking

Hillsborough, North Carolina

www.handtoolwoodworking.com

Elia Bizzarri says he always knew he wanted to make furniture. His parents built him a small shop when he was sixteen. When he was seventeen, he began an apprenticeship with Curtis Buchanan, a giant in the world of Windsor-chair making. "Curtis is a generous man, a skilled chair maker, and a naturally gifted teacher," Bizzarri tells me. "It was a very easy way to become a craftsman."

Bizzarri met the chair maker Peter Galbert in 2006 at a conference on woodworking in the eighteenth century, held at Colonial Williamsburg. Galbert showed him a travisher he had designed and suggested Bizzarri make one. He did.

Today, most of the toolmaking for Bizzarri's company falls to Seth Elliott, who has worked with Bizzarri since 2017. Bizzarri concentrates on teaching and making custom-order Windsor chairs. Elliott makes the travishers in batches of fifty, working with O1 tool steel blades from three suppliers. He shapes the sole of each body to conform to a specific blade. "Our goal is to make fifty that all cut and that all cut the same," Elliott tells me. Bizzarri sells travishers with either a 4 ½-inch or a 12-inch radius.

North Carolina chair maker Elia Bizzarri sells a
Galbert-style travisher. His associate, Seth Elliott,
does most of the fabricating.

Profile: Peter Galbert

In the close-knit world of Windsor-chair making, a few names stand out. One is Peter Galbert, who has been making Windsors, teaching others to make them, writing about Windsors, and inventing tools for more than twenty years.

Before Galbert knew that he had found his calling, though, he spent a good ten years sorting through the lumber pile of life to find the right career board. He tried the School of the Art Institute of Chicago. "I was doing drawing, painting, sculpture, photography, and I always had a fondness for the woodshop," he tells me. "I did drop out. I'm not really a terrible painter, but I knew it wasn't for me."

Galbert moved to New York City in the late 1990s to pursue that fondness for wood. "There was a lot of money around and a lot of work. You could basically pick what you wanted to do and do it." Galbert tried working for galleries, then for cabinetmaking shops, then for the New York venue of the National Museum of the American Indian. But nothing clicked. Then he rented a small shop that he shared with someone making arch-top guitars. "It was very eye opening to see what he could do in very little space," Galbert tells

me. "It was what we all thought woodworking was going to be—shaping wood."

Galbert finally found his calling in 1999, when he made his first chair. "It was amazing. I was making wood into something," he says. "Before, I was just trying to make a blade follow a path. Now, all of a sudden, I was sculpting. I was learning to turn. I had no instruction in any of those things. I was making it up as I went."

A couple of years later, after taking a class with the Windsor master Curtis Buchanan, Galbert began teaching with Buchanan, then conducting classes on his own. He's taught at many of the leading woodworking and craft schools in the United States, including the North Bennet Street School in Boston.

Today, Galbert spends most of his time in his shop/classroom in a renovated mill building on the Salmon Falls River in Rollinsford, New Hampshire. His classes cover every aspect of chair making, from splitting logs to final assembly. The teaching and making feed off each other, he says. "Nothing's a chore. It's a pleasure when I can dive into making a chair. Teaching teaches me how makers make. I spend my time learning things."

After years of woodworking, Peter Galbert found his true calling as a Windsor-chair maker. Here, he leads a class at his school in New Hampshire.

Crown Plane

South Portland, Maine
www.crownplane.com

James S. White learned to make travishers and wood-bodied planes because his father took a class in Windsor-chair making from Mike Dunbar of the Windsor Institute. That's how White met Leon E. Robbins, a New England original who, in the guise of Crown Plane, made tools for Dunbar's school. When Robbins became too frail to continue his business, White bought it. "I learned the trade from Leon and have kept it going for twenty-two years," White tells me.

White says he's always been around tools, thanks to his father, who practiced metalworking, woodworking, and gunsmithing in his spare time. "I knew from the start that I wasn't cut out to work in an office. I've always been working with my hands." So, he says, "I went to prep school and after graduation slid right into a machine shop." He eventually went to college, earning a degree in history.

Today, White works in a large nineteenth-century mercantile building in South Portland, Maine. He shares the space with his brother's pottery-making shop and his wife's vintage-goods business. His band rehearses on the second floor. The shop equipment includes a workbench he built as well as the one his father used, two band saws, a Bridgeport planer/jointer, plus grinders and sanders.

White gets tempered o1 tool steel blanks for his travisher irons from a friend at a local machine shop. He bends them and grinds the edges. He makes the travisher's wood bodies from hard maple, with an ebony wear strip added to the sole. White's travisher is similar to the ones that Bizzarri and Minihan make. But, at 6 ½ inches long, White's blade is longer, and the handles on his tool aren't as fluid and sculptural.

It takes him about a day to make a single travisher, but he generally makes them in small batches. "I love to have stuff in stock, but I never do," he says. He sells his tools through Woodcraft and Highland Hardware, as well as on the Etsy website (www.etsy.com/shop/CrownPlane).

Working under the Crown Plane banner, James White
makes travishers and hand planes to order. The bodies
are hard maple, with an ebony wear strip.

The Windsor Workshop
West Chiltington, West Sussex, England
www.thewindsorworkshop.co.uk

In 1996, James Mursell was running his family's fruit farm in West Sussex, England. Then he took a course in chair making at the prestigious West Dean College, which would steer his career in a very different direction. As he tells me, "Two years after I made that first chair, when I couldn't make chairs as elegantly as I wanted, I spent a week studying with Mike Dunbar, who introduced me to green woodworking and the beauty of American Windsors. I became obsessed with Windsors, and I decided to try to make a business out of making chairs. I did that for three years. Then the college where I made my first chair asked me to run the program. I have three strands to my business—teaching, making the chairs, and making the tools."

The toolmaking began with an accident: Mursell dropped the travisher he had been using and broke it. "I needed something rough and ready quickly for a course I was teaching," he says. "I roughed out the shape from a piece of sycamore. It seemed to work well, and I started teaching with it."

That rough and ready shape resembles a flattened kidney bean with a blade sticking out of one side. It couldn't be more different from the travisher that Claire Minihan produces. "I've always liked speed," Mursell says. "Time is a key ingredient. I want tools that go to work really fast. I wanted a tool that would rip off the wood and give a pretty good finish. But the finish from my travisher is probably not as good as from Claire's."

These days, Mursell has suppliers do nearly all the manufacturing for his travisher. Ben Orford of Craft Lab (page 204) has made the blades for more than fifteen years. A CNC milling operation now shapes the bodies. Mursell says he's more involved in making the two styles of spokeshaves he sells.

Initially, Mursell used only hard maple for the travisher's body. But then, a few years ago, he wanted to add a premium model, with "a lump of brass on the sole." The CNC operation found it couldn't get a crisp edge in wood on the pocket for the brass. It suggested shaping the body from a thermoplastic called Delrin. "They made a prototype and it was fabulous," Mursell says.

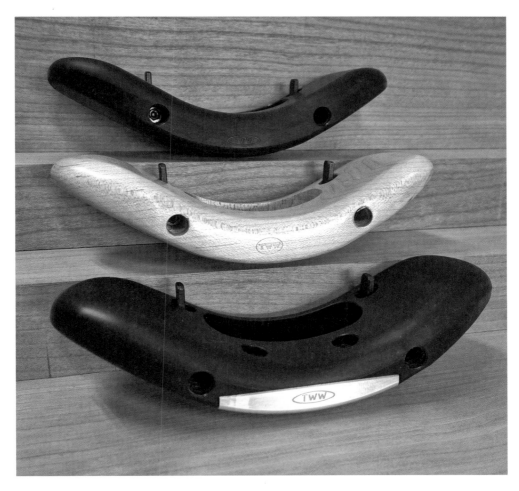

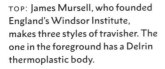

TOP: James Mursell, who founded England's Windsor Institute, makes three styles of travisher. The one in the foreground has a Delrin thermoplastic body.

ABOVE LEFT: Mursell says his travishers are designed to remove wood rapidly. "I've always liked speed," he says.

ABOVE RIGHT: Once in charge of his family's fruit farm, Mursell now makes Windsor chairs, teaches chair making, and makes tools.

Profile: Russ Filbeck

Spokeshave maker Russ Filbeck learned from the best. He studied woodturning with Jerry Glaser, one of the towering figures in the craft. Brian Boggs and Mike Dunbar, two of the finest craftsmen in the United States, introduced Filbeck to chair making. That started him down a path of paying things forward—charitable work that connected him with former president Jimmy Carter and back to a home for troubled boys that he knew from his youth.

Filbeck, a Navy veteran, retired from the service in the mid-1980s and started a furniture-restoration business while earning two degrees from San Diego State University. As soon as he graduated, he began to teach woodworking at Palomar College in San Diego.

Six years later, he took a week-long class with Brian Boggs, learning how to make a ladder back chair from green wood. Soon after that, he drove to New Hampshire to take two Windsor-chair classes with Mike Dunbar. "I was so excited about green woodworking that I immediately began writing the curriculum to teach two courses in it," he says.

In 2004, to prepare for writing the book *Making Ladder Back Chairs*, Filbeck began researching the chairs' history. He interviewed Boggs, Jennie Alexander, Roy Underhill, and other artisans making Appalachian-style ladder back chairs and asked them each to write a page about their techniques.

"I knew that President Carter had taught himself how to make a ladder back chair after he left the White House. I said to my wife, Carol, 'Wouldn't it be great if I could get President Carter to write a page, too.'" He contacted the Carter Center and soon talked with the former president. As Filbeck tells the story, Carter remarked that "everyone wants to talk politics, but no one wants to talk about making chairs."

In 2005, Filbeck made a cherry ladder back rocking chair for Carter and a set of Shaker oval boxes for Rosalynn Carter. A year after delivering those gifts, he began donating his work to the annual charity auction for the Carter Center. Today, his pieces fetch six-figure bids there.

Filbeck's normally firm voice cracks when he talks about his connection with the Good Samaritan Boys Ranch, near Springfield, Missouri. "In December 1959, I was a fourteen-year-old runaway," he says. "The sheriff who caught me gave me a choice: the reformatory or this ranch." Filbeck chose the ranch, but planned to flee as soon as he could. That quickly changed. "I was the only kid who had grown up on a farm, so I knew how to milk cows and how to separate calves from their mothers. The first week, I wound up with a damn job and forgot to run away." He adds, "The ranch did its job in turning me around."

Filbeck returns to the ranch each summer to teach chair making and Shaker box making. The ranch built him a spacious shop building, and colleagues from the San Diego Fine Woodworkers Association donated truckloads of tools and machinery.

Today, Filbeck works in half of a two-car garage stuffed with a Robust lathe, two large band saws, a fifteen-inch planer, his workbench, a shave horse, and the Craftsman table saw he bought in 1968. There, he teaches chair making and shapes spokeshaves from a wide variety of exotic woods. He says a concave bronze spokeshave that Brian Boggs designed inspired him to design his own in wood, using blades from Ron Hock (page 139).

"I moved the handles to the bottom and the front of the wooden body, in line with the cutter, so the tool doesn't roll," he explains. "With other spokeshaves, you have to use your wrists to keep it from rolling. Mine eliminates all the wrist stress and torque."

Many of the dozens of woods Filbeck uses have a backstory. The black acacia comes from San Diego's old Naval Training Center, for instance. The Osage orange grew on his family's farm in Missouri. The purpleheart was taken from the keel of the San Salvador, a sailing ship built in San Diego. The ancient kauri, which is some 50,000 years old, was unearthed in New Zealand.

He sells the spokeshaves on his website (russfilbeck.com) as well as at Lie-Nielsen Hand Tool Events throughout the West.

ABOVE LEFT: Russ Filbeck watches as a new generation of chair makers manipulates one of his spokeshaves.

ABOVE RIGHT: For his spokeshave bodies, Filbeck uses eleven different hardwoods, including ancient kauri, pink myrtle, yew, boxwood, bocote, and ebony.

LEFT: After retiring from the Navy, Filbeck settled in San Diego, where he makes chairs and tools in a small and very crowded shop.

Adzes, Hatchets,
and Knives

MORE THAN OTHER ARTISANS, carvers and people who work with green wood can transform a board, branch, or log into something that transcends the tree. A crooked branch becomes a spoon or a ladle. A freshly cut log can be hollowed for a bowl or split, hewn, and assembled into a piece of furniture. With knives in the right hands, a piece of basswood can be transformed into anything from a comic figure to a graceful acanthus leaf. And just as the types of carving range from the ridiculous to the sublime, carving tools themselves cover an equally wide range.

Adzes and hatchets are the big guns, used to chop away large amounts of wood in a hurry to rough shape a bowl, a spoon, or a large figure. Knives add the details. Knives with short, straight blades can handle many styles of carving: duck decoys, Native American–style totems, caricature carving, and more. Knives with a blade bent into a semicircle are generally for making a hollow in the wood, as for a spoon or a ladle. Gouges or V-shaped tools are for elaborate relief carving. European factories dominate that latter part of the carving-tool market. I found only one American maker with those tools in his lineup.

I'm not a wood-carver or a green woodworker, so I don't have personal experience to help me identify good carving tools—especially adzes. So I spoke with David Fisher, a well-known bowl carver, to learn what he wants from a good tool. "The most important part of an adze is the bevel and the relationship between the handle and the shape of the head," he says. "The bevel is much more critical because of the nature of the swing. With an ax, the edge is in line with your swing, so you're able to adjust a bit to vary how the bevel contacts the wood. With an adze, you have to totally change your swing. It's like swinging a hoe. If the head is too closed, it will dig in, and if it's too open, it won't cut the weeds at all."

Fisher also explains how to do a test to check the geometry of the adze. "If I put the adze on the bench," he says, "the cutting edge should be perpendicular where it will enter the bench. If it's heading backward, I'll be slamming the bevel into the wood, and that's going to hurt."

Fisher also has some general advice about carving knives. He says he prefers blades made with carbon steel because, compared to other alloys, carbon steel delivers a sharper edge and is easy to hone once it dulls.

When you sharpen an edge tool, like a knife, moving the blade over an abrasive stone rolls a sliver of metal. This is known as the wire edge. Fisher says you have to sharpen and hone until the wire edge "comes off like a silver hair."

Kjetil Groven, a Norwegian-born toolmaker, has another key piece of advice. "Most blades in the United States are related to hunting," he tells me. "But in Norway, a knife is a tool. It's important that it isn't a weapon."

ABOVE LEFT: Spoon carving has become a fairly popular pastime, and several makers produce curved-blade knives for this craft.

ABOVE RIGHT: Think of an adze as a hatchet turned sideways. It's designed to remove a lot of wood in a hurry for bowl carving and other work.

LEFT: Several knife makers get their steel from old sources, such as spent sawmill blades.

Jason A. Lonon Toolmaker

Marion, North Carolina
jasonlonon.ecwid.com

When Jason Lonon was sixteen years old, he talked his way into an apprenticeship with the master furniture maker Hugh Bowman. "Hugh had retired and didn't think he wanted to take on any more apprentices," Lonon says. "But I kind of twisted his arm and hung around his shop long enough. This was one of the formative experiences of my life. It was wonderful to spend so much time side by side at the bench."

The apprenticeship focused on furniture making, followed by a period of dulcimer making. (Lonon plays, and cut two records with his sister and brother.) But at the start of the 2000s, Lonon launched his career as a blacksmith and toolmaker. Over the years, he's made a variety of forged tools. By early 2016, he put aside everything to focus on making adzes. "I sell them as fast as I can make them," he says. In 2019, he also began making hatchets and carving knives.

He forges the adze and hatchet heads from 4140 steel, a tough metal with good impact resistance. He uses O1 tool steel for his knife blades.

Today, Lonon works in a small town east of Asheville, North Carolina, in a shop that holds antique power hammers, grinders, a forge, and anvils, as well as some woodworking equipment. He works with Justin Boling, a childhood friend, and Paul Clark, his brother-in-law. Boling handles grinding and finishing; Clark, knife making. The three usually work in their own shops, coordinating to produce a unified line of tools.

"We have a kind of family business inspired by the old cottage industries," Lonon tells me. "If you work only by yourself, you can only get so far. I've found it valuable to have talented people working side by side. There's a saying: one horse can pull a thousand pounds, but two horses can pull five thousand pounds. The three of us together are doing more than three individuals can do."

TOP: Working with two associates, Jason Lonon makes knives, adzes, drawknives, and hatchets in a shop filled with antique equipment.

ABOVE LEFT: Lonon's bowl adzes have a blade with an elliptical sweep and turned-up corners. He says this allows for aggressive cutting yet leaves a smooth finish.

ABOVE RIGHT: Lonon makes ten different knives, both curved and straight, with handles of maple, oak, cherry, or walnut.

Stark Raven Studios

Hurley, Wisconsin
www.stark-raven-studios.com

Dan Roesinger, the metalworking half of Stark Raven Studios, says of smithing, "There's an elemental draw to it, like staring into the coals of a campfire. Then there's the ability to transform material, along with the technical challenge of forming a rigid material into something different."

In 1997, Roesinger left his teaching job and began making rustic furniture. Two years later, a friend introduced him to blacksmithing. The two began collecting tools at flea markets, and Roesinger built a forge in his backyard. But, he says, "within two months, blacksmithing had become a sideline." In the summer of 2002, he shifted entirely to blacksmithing.

The other half of Stark Raven Studios is Roesinger's wife, Saga Erickson. She is an artist who sometimes helps in the forge as a striker. That means, for example, that he leads with blows from a lightweight hammer, showing her where to strike with a heavy two-handed sledgehammer.

Roesinger says the couple "try to keep our life simple and humble," living in a small house on an acre of land outside a small town in northern Wisconsin. The shop, in a small log building, holds Roesinger's homemade forge, two anvils and a Mayer Brothers power hammer that was probably made between 1915 and 1920. When he began Stark Raven Studios, Roesinger made his own charcoal to fuel the forge; now, because of his "overwhelming backlog," he uses coke. "As soon as I'm able to do so, I'll go back to making charcoal," he says.

Much of the steel Roesinger uses is recycled, which minimizes the environmental impact of his work, but also presents a challenge. "There are stresses in recycled metal," he says. "There might also be some fine cracks. You're going to find out as you forge it." To minimize these problems, Roesinger heats the steel to between fourteen hundred and fifteen hundred degrees, when it turns cherry red. Then he lets the steel cool slowly. After three heatings and coolings, the stresses have usually relaxed. "The process can't repair cracks already present, so you still get unwelcome surprises sometimes," Roesinger explains. When he hardens and tempers the steel, he leaves it slightly harder than most other axes,

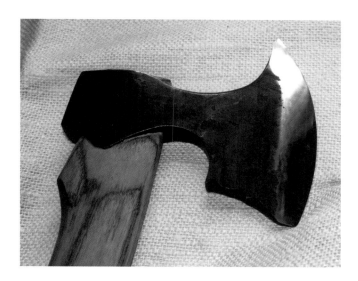

ABOVE: Dan Roesinger, of Stark Raven Studios, makes a large and small carving hatchet with a fierce-looking head that follows traditional Scandinavian designs.

LEFT: Roesinger and his wife, Saga Erickson, live and work in a wooded area outside a small northern Wisconsin town.

because his tools are meant for controlled carving in green wood, not the heavy pounding that a general-purpose hatchet would see.

Roesinger makes his hatchet heads by forge welding recycled metal to a piece of new W1 steel, with the material "screaming hot." Once the head is shaped, hardened, and tempered, he grinds its edge to a fairly steep bevel of about twenty-three degrees. He also bends the cutting edge slightly, so it kicks out a little at the bottom. This makes it easier to carve with the hatchet, he says. "I like to be able to shave with a finished ax head," he says, "and see a pretty clear reflection in the bevel." It takes Roesinger about a day and a half to forge a hatchet head, shape the handle, and make a blade cover.

"It's important to me to work in a way that reflects my values," Roesinger says. "I think we need to pay close attention to the climate crisis. My carbon footprint is very small, and I can make my shop carbon neutral or carbon negative. But I can't make the manufacture of the steel carbon neutral. The best thing for me is to use steel from a junkyard."

Cariboo Blades

Williams Lake, British Columbia, Canada

www.caribooblades.com

In 1997, Scott Richardson and Aki Yamamoto moved north from Vancouver to the remote Cariboo/Chilcotin region of British Columbia. There, they live off the grid ("Every time we move the outhouse we plant an apple tree"), relying on solar power for their home and knife-making business.

For adze blades, they say, "The steel is cut and forged from six-foot- and five-foot-diameter saw blades. The carbon steel saw blades we collected twenty years ago from local lumber mills. We forge spring steel adze blades recovering 5160 spring steel from older auto wrecks. For larger, heavier half-inch-thick adze blades, spring steel is an excellent high-carbon steel."

The Cariboo Blades shop consists of a skeleton of thick logs sheathed in plastic sheeting. "We work with the sun and choose to use hand tools as much as we can instead of machines. We try to recover every material used in building our tools and knives." They maintain that "there is enough high-carbon steel and recoverable material, of the highest quality, for every knife and toolmaker to be supplied for life."

Richardson and Yamamoto produce a line of adzes and carving knives, most made to order.

TOP: The couple working as Cariboo Blades rely on solar power and recycled metal to make adzes, drawknives, and other tools to order.

BOTTOM: You can order a knife from Cariboo with a handle made from reclaimed wood, or order just a blade and add a handle of your own design.

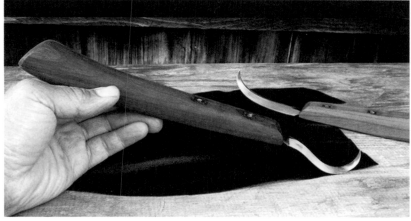

Brent Bailey Forge

Orland, California

www.brentbaileyforge.com

In 1998, Brent Bailey was living in a trailer on his father's 110-acre ranch in Northern California and working nights at a bar. An acquaintance kindled his interest in blacksmithing. That interest ignited when a magazine article led Bailey to a training course in Zimbabwe. He learned the craft there and in Mozambique, then spent several years teaching in Peru, Australia, and South Africa.

At first, he specialized in making ornamental pieces that he sold through The Blacksmith Shop and its gallery, in Ferndale, California—the largest complex in the United States devoted to forged iron work.

With the birth of his son in 2013, Bailey says, "Everything changed. I had to get more serious about my work and about making a lot more money." Today, he operates Brent Bailey Forge, specializing in hammers and hatchets. He uses a variety of steel in his tools, including w2 ("it holds an edge very well," he says) and 6150 steel. Bailey sells a small ax, which he named Carry Me, that can work as a carving hatchet.

He still lives and works on that 110-acre ranch. His shop holds a large trip hammer, a coal forge, a few grinders, and a few hammers. "People come into my shop and say, 'Wow! This is it?' It's a pretty simple setup."

This carving hatchet is one of several that Brent Bailey forges in his Northern California shop.

North Bay Forge
Waldron Island, Washington
www.northbayforge.com

The love of sea kayaking drew Jim Wester and his wife to settle on Waldron Island, Washington, a dot of land near the Canadian border, in the mid-1980s. They went on a long voyage with friends, who sailed in a dory instead of kayaks. "I fell in love with that dory," Wester says. "I couldn't find one for sale at a reasonable price, so I built one." That took him two years and led him to a toolmaker named Dick Anderson. Wester set up an informal apprenticeship with Anderson, which lasted about a year and a half. After that, Wester outfitted a shop and set himself up in the knife-making business as North Bay Forge.

Today, three decades later, he's still making carving knives and adzes from w1 steel, which he quenches in oil. "It's very forgiving," Wester says. He forges and finishes the knife blades individually. He makes several elbow adzes, which have the steel head lashed to an L-shaped wood handle, and a bowl adze that's solid steel with wood scales riveted to the handle.

In addition to a full range of carving knives, North Bay Forge makes elbow adzes, with a blade lashed to a crooked piece of eastern cherry.

Drake Knives

Arlington, Washington

drake-knives.myshopify.com

Like many others profiled in this book, Gil Drake began his career with making knives out of frustration. "I became interested in wood carving about twenty years ago," he says, "and I had trouble finding tools that would hold an edge and that weren't super expensive. So I decided to try making my own. I took them to several knife shows and sold them out of a little tackle box for a while." The business outgrew the tackle box long ago. Now, Drake Knives sells a line of forty-one tools online and at three to four wood-carving shows per year.

Drake lives and works in Arlington, Washington, about fifty miles north of Seattle. He runs his business with his wife and oldest son. "I do all the blade work," he says. The shop holds a multitude of grinders—eight belt grinders and twenty to thirty bench grinders, each with wheels shaped for a specific tool. Drake says, "I forge all my tools. We don't outsource anything. " Drake uses O1 tool steel for his sweeps and gouges, 1095 spring steel for the knife blades. Buyers can get free sharpening for life. He makes batches of tools, twenty-five to fifty at a time. "It does not get boring. I enjoy making tools so much," he says.

RIGHT: Gil Drake (in the white hat) began making his own tools when he couldn't find ones that performed the way he wanted.

FACING PAGE, FROM THE TOP: Among the forty-three knives that Drake makes are a curved spoon-carver, a V tool for decorative carving, and a knife with a sheep's-foot blade for heavy cutting.

Craft Lab

Herefordshire, West Midlands, England
benandloisorford.com

The English blade maker Ben Orford began his career with a three-year apprenticeship in green woodworking, followed by courses in cabinet-making and furniture design. "I could find old tools and fix them up, but I started making my own tools for my own use," he tells me. "People would see what I was using, and when they found out I'd made the tool, they'd ask me to make one for them."

Orford has been making knives since 2003. He works with his wife, Lois, who is also a trained green woodworker. These days, she sews the leather sheaths for the knives that Orford forges.

The Orfords call their shop the Craft Lab. About half the Orfords' output are Bushcraft knives for the outdoors, half carving knives. "The standard knives are made from 01 tool steel, which is a high carbon tool steel which means it needs a bit more care than a stainless steel knife, but to my mind is superior because it is easier to sharpen, has a good edge holding ability, and feels nicer to use," says the company's website. "We do make knives from other steels, including various stainless steels, D2, and Damascus steels," Orford adds.

TOP: Ben Orford is one of several knifesmiths who make a general-purpose knife called a sloyd. Orford's has a blade of 01 steel epoxied into an elm handle.

BOTTOM: Orford calls this an engraving knife. The blade is just an inch long, making it well suited for adding fine detail to a carving.

Pinewood Forge

Leonard, Minnesota

pinewoodforge.com

In 1989, Del Stubbs was teaching woodturning seminars in Europe. He shifted his focus to wood carving after spending a winter with the Swedish master carver Wille Sundqvist, learning from him the richness of traditional woodcraft.

Stubbs began attending spoon-carving gatherings in Minnesota. This led him to knife making, and he began producing small batches of knives for friends. It wasn't long before he was making knives full time. In 2000, he founded Pinewood Forge specifically to make the type of knives that Swedish folk artists use.

At first, Stubbs set up shop in a shed. "It was thousands of degrees on the side with the forge, but twenty below on the other side," he says. He has since built a larger, more comfortable shop, where he works, he says, eighty to one hundred hours a week. Making a hook knife involves about seventy separate operations: heat-treating, shaping, grinding, polishing, and so on.

Stubbs buys 01 tool steel for his blades from a smelter in Austria. An elbow injury several years ago put a end to his forging. Now, he has a supplier laser cut blanks, which he heat-treats and tempers. He uses a salt bath for the tempering. "I can control the temperature to within one degree, and that's better for the steel since it never sees oxygen," Stubbs says.

Stubbs figures that he makes about two thousand knives a year. "The romance of pounding on steel is about one percent of the work," he says. "You have to be obsessed with the person you're working for. So every time I touch a piece of steel I'm making a tool for a good friend."

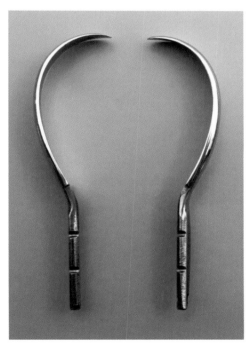

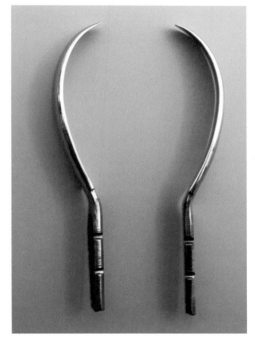

TOP: A hook knife and a sloyd knife from Del Stubbs at Pinewood Forge. Many of his blades have a very pronounced hook for hollowing a spoon bowl.

ABOVE: Stubbs also sells blades alone, for people who want to add their own handles. These are a number 1 (left) and number 2 (right) sweep, in left-hand and right-hand versions.

Preferred Edge Carving Knives & Supplies
Camrose, Alberta, Canada
www.preferrededge.ca

Bruce Bernard, the owner of Preferred Edge Carving Knives & Supplies, died as this book was being prepared for press. His company has since stopped taking new orders. The story of Bernard and his company is still worth telling, for they filled a unique niche in the world of knife making.

Preferred Edge is a portal to the world of Northwest coastal indigenous carving. This type of carving produces masks, amulets, and totems shaped into the stylized forms of eagles, frogs, fish, and other creatures. The curved surfaces of the carvings are smooth, the features usually accentuated with paint. Following the links on the Preferred Edge website leads to a wealth of information about prominent carvers and their work.

Bruce Bernard took over Preferred Edge in 2010, trading in a career as a heavy-duty mechanic for the much smaller mechanics of knife making. He does a lot of business with the schools in British Columbia, saying, "The school system is committed to teaching indigenous carving." He also works with prison inmates who want to learn carving.

Bernard has a supplier cut knife blanks with a water jet from recycled band saw blades made from 15N20 steel. This is a high-carbon steel, so it sharpens easily. Bernard grinds the blades with a jig and then files and sharpens the blades by hand. He tempers the steel and hones the cutting edges. "I have two heat-treating ovens," he tells me. "I heat the steel for twenty minutes and quench it in oil. Then I temper it to HRC 58." He says of his process, "I want consistency in the shape and quality, but at the same time I don't want to be McDonald's."

Bernard says that a knife's edge and its bevel make the difference between an ordinary tool and a good one. "If it's a really fine knife, you'll get a glossy finish on end grain like you get with a plane."

The Preferred Edge catalog lists more than fifty knives. The company also sells five adzes.

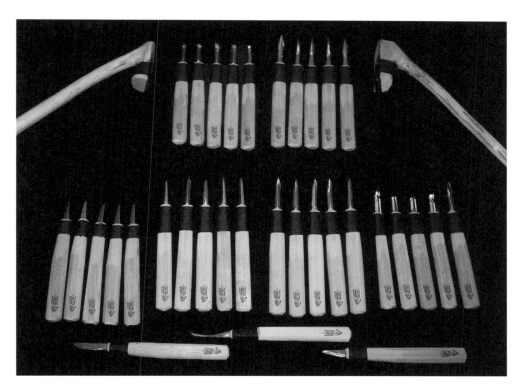

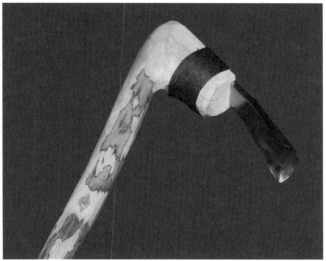

The lineup from Preferred Edge: more than fifty different knives and five adzes, including the elbow adze shown at the left.

Deepwoods Ventures

Bemidji, Minnesota
deepwoodsventures.com

Paul Jones has been making knives since he was a teenager. His father, a maintenance worker, would bring home used hacksaw blades that Jones shaped into knives. "I found more joy in making the tool than in using it," he tells me. Decades later, he decided to prune his knife collection by selling the surplus on eBay. "They sold immediately," he says. "People contacted me and asked if I'd make more. So I got busy and made one here and made one there. It soon became more expensive to stay at my marketing job than to stay at home and make knives." So, in 2013, Jones left and launched Deepwoods Ventures.

He works in a modest shop in Bemidji, Minnesota, using w1 drill rod for his blades. Jones says, "I like w1 because it's more forgiving in the heat-treating." The W in the steel's name indicates it can be quenched in water. However, Jones quenches the steel in peanut oil. "Quenching in water was problematic for me. And quenching in oil makes for a tougher blade."

Jones says he can forge as many as sixty-five to eighty blades a day and give them one tempering. A second tempering has to wait until the next day. He works fourteen-hour days, six days a week. He says, "I'll do six days and take time off to go to church."

TOP: Paul Jones, of Deepwoods Ventures, makes his knife blades from drill rod that he tempers twice.

CENTER: Jones offers his Skinny Sloyd knife in three blade lengths and a choice of plain or figured wood for the handle.

BOTTOM: The spoon hook carver from Deepwoods Ventures has an eight-inch handle in oak or tiger maple.

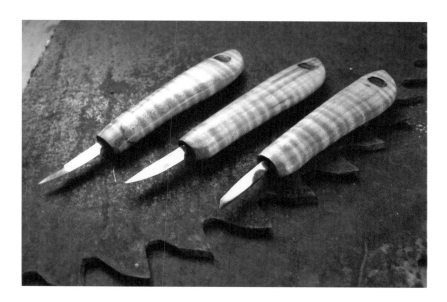

Index of Makers

A note on tools and products:
One $ indicates a very low price range;
$$, a low range; and so on up to $$$$$—
a very high price range.

Prominent Toolworks

Bridge City Tool Works
bridgecitytools.com
page 25

Lee Valley and Veritas Tools
www.leevalley.com/en-ca
www.veritastools.com
page 20

Lie-Nielsen Toolworks
www.lie-nielsen.com
page 14

Woodpeckers
www.woodpeck.com
page 30

Workbenches

Acer-Ferrous Toolworks
redrosereproductions.com
▸ vise components $–$$
page 54

Benchcrafted
www.benchcrafted.com
▸ benches $$$$, vises and hardware $$
page 38

Blum Tool Co.
blumtool.com
▸ cabinetmakers bench $$$$,
  portable bench $$$
page 56

Frank Strazza
www.strazzafurniture.com
▸ benches $$$$$
page 46

Lake Erie Toolworks
www.lakeerietoolworks.com
▸ vise kits $$, benches $$$$
page 52

Plate 11 Woodworking
www.plate11.com
▸ benches $$$$–$$$$$
page 42

RE-CO BKLYN
www.recobklyn.com
▸ bench kit $$$$
page 48

Texas Heritage Woodworks
www.txheritage.net
▸ vise components $–$$
page 55

Squares, Gauges, Marking Knives, and Awls

Blackburn Tools
www.blackburntools.com
▸ scrawl $
page 71

Blue Spruce Toolworks
bluesprucetoolworks.com
▸ squares and bevel gauges $$,
  marking knives $, awl $
page 68

Bridge City Tool Works
bridgecitytools.com
▸ universal gauge $$
page 70

Colen Clenton
www.instagram.com/colenclenton
▸ measuring and marking tools $$–$$$
page 62

Czeck Edge Hand Tool
www.czeckedge.com
▸ birdcage awl $, ruler stop $
page 78

DFM Tool Works
dfmtoolworks.com
▸ square $, marking knives $–$$, dowel plate $
page 76

Florip Toolworks
www.floriptoolworks.com
▸ marking gauge $$
page 74

Glen-Drake Toolworks
www.glen-drake.com
▸ marking gauges $–$$
page 72

Hamilton Toolworks
www.hamiltontools.com
▸ marking knife $$, marking gauges $–$$
page 75

Seth Gould
www.sethgould.com
▸ dividers and calipers $$
page 77

Shenandoah Tool Works
www.shenandoahtoolworks.com
▸ birdcage awl $
page 71

Sterling Tool Works
www.sterlingtoolworks.com
▸ dovetail square $
page 71

Vesper Tools
www.vespertools.com.au
▸ bevel gauges and squares $$,
   marking knives $–$$
page 66

Hand Saws

Bad Axe Tool Works
www.badaxetoolworks.com
▸ saws $$
page 88

Florip Toolworks
www.floriptoolworks.com
▸ saws $$
page 92

Skelton Saws
www.skeltonsaws.co.uk
▸ saws $$–$$$$
page 82

Tools for Working Wood
www.toolsforworkingwood.com
▸ saw kits $, saws $$
page 96

Hand Planes

Benedetto
www.benedettoguitars.com
▸ hand planes $$
page 148

Bill Carter
www.billcarterwoodworkingplanemaker.co.uk
▸ hand planes $$–$$$$
page 120

BJS Planes and Woodworking
www.bjsplanesandwoodworking.com
▸ hand planes $$$$
page 122

Blum Tool Co.
blumtool.com
▸ hand planes $$–$$$, sharpening box $$
page 142

Brese Plane
breseplane.blogspot.com
▸ hand planes $$$$
page 118

Bridge City Tool Works
bridgecitytools.com
▸ hand planes $$$
page 143

Daed Toolworks
www.daedtoolworks.com
▸ hand planes $$$$
page 116

HNT Gordon & Co.
www.hntgordon.com.au
▸ hand planes $$–$$$, half set of hollows
   and rounds $$$$
page 144

Holtey Classic Hand Planes
www.holteyplanes.com
▸ hand planes $$$$–$$$$$
page 106

J. Wilding
www.jwildingplanemaker.com
▸ hand planes $$
page 134

PUBLISHED BY
Princeton Architectural Press
202 Warren Street, Hudson
New York 12534
www.papress.com

© 2021 David Heim
All rights reserved.
Printed and bound in China
24 23 22 21 4 3 2 1 First edition

ISBN 978-1-61689-924-0

ACQUIRING EDITOR: Jan Hartman
PROJECT EDITOR: Clare Jacobson
DESIGNER: Paul Wagner

Every reasonable attempt has been made to identify owners of copyright. Errors or omissions will be corrected in subsequent editions.

Library of Congress Cataloging-in-Publication Data is available from the publisher.

CREDITS:
pp. 13, 14, 17, 59, 61, 65, 74, 87, 91, 92, 96, 97, 100, 101, 129, 130, 136–138, 180, Author. pp. 19, 37, Lie-Nielsen Toolworks. pp. 21–24, Lee Valley and Veritas Tools. pp. 26, 29, 70, 143, Joe Felzman. pp. 31, 32, Woodpeckers. pp. 39–41, 50, 51, Benchcrafted. pp. 43, 44, Plate 11 Woodworking. p. 45, Chris Schwarz. pp. 46, 47, Frank Strazza. p. 49, RE-CO BKLYN. pp. 52–53, Lake Erie Toolworks. pp. 54, 140, 141, Red Rose Reproductions. p. 55, Texas Heritage Woodworks. pp. 57, 142, 163 bottom, Blum Tool Co. pp. 63 top & lower left, 98, Tools for Working Wood. pp. 63 lower right, 64 left, 144, 145, 163 top, 178, HNT Gordon & Co. p. 64 right, Colen Clenton. pp. 66, 67, Chris Vesper. pp. 69, 158, Blue Spruce Toolworks. pp. 71 top & second from top, 162, Sterling Tool Works. pp. 71 third from top, 161, Shenandoah Tool Works. p. 71 bottom, Blackburn Tools. p. 73, Glen-Drake Toolworks. p. 75, Hamilton Toolworks. p. 76, DFM Tool Works. pp. 77, 164, Seth Gould. p. 79, Czeck Edge Hand Tools. pp. 82–85, Jacqueline Skelton. pp. 89, 90, Bad Axe Toolworks. pp. 94, 95, Marco Terenzi. p. 104 top & center, M.S. Bickford. pp. 104 bottom, 114, 115, The Lazarus Handplane Co. pp. 106–8, Karl Holtey. pp. 111, 112, Sauer & Steiner. p. 113, Jameel Abraham. pp. 116, 117, Daed Toolworks. pp. 119, 168, Brese Planes. p. 121, Bill Carter. p. 123, BJS Planes and Woodworking. pp. 125–27, Old Street Tool. p. 131, St. James Bay Tool Company. pp. 132–33, Philly Planes. pp. 134–35, Micah Wilding. p. 139, Ron Hock. pp. 146, 147, Scott Meek Woodworks. pp. 148, 149, Cindy Benedetto. pp. 150–52, Walke Moore Tools. p. 153, Kevin Shea. pp. 154, 165, 200, Brent Bailey Forge. pp. 155–57, 165, 181, Old Soldier Toolworks. p. 159, Scott Landis, GreenWood. p. 160, Lost Art Press. pp. 167, 180, Barr Specialty Tools. p. 169, Elkhead Tools. pp. 171 top, 185, Peter Galbert. pp. 171 bottom, 193 top left, 195, Jason A. Lonon Toolmaker. p. 173, Caleb James Maker. pp. 174, 175, Carolyn Wachnicki. p. 177, Moberg Tools. pp. 179, 193 top right & bottom, 199, Cariboo Blades. p. 183, Claire Minihan Woodworks. p. 184, Alec Himwich. p. 187, James S. White. p. 189, The Windsor Workshop. p. 191, Russ Filbeck. p. 197, Stark Raven Studios. p. 201, North Bay Forge. pp. 202, 203, Drake Knives. p. 205, Craft Lab. p. 207, Pinewood Forge. p. 209, Preferred Edge Carving Knives & Supplies. p. 211, Deepwoods Ventures.

ON PAGE 2:
FIRST ROW: Tools for Working Wood, Jason A. Lonon Toolmaker, Brese Planes / SECOND ROW: Author, Walke Moore Tools, Benchcrafted / THIRD ROW: Chris Vesper, Joe Felzman, Claire Minihan Woodworks / FOURTH ROW: BJS Planes and Woodworking, Lee Valley and Veritas Tools, Shenandoah Tool Works / FIFTH ROW: HNT Gordon & Co., Brese Planes, Micah Wilding

ON THE COVER CLOCKWISE FROM TOP LEFT:
Clockwise from top left: Jason A. Lonon Toolmaker, Joe Felzman, David Heim, Russ Filbeck